Shadows and Shields: The Journey of a Cybersecurity Visionary

Dedication

To those who dared to dream beyond the shadows, who built their shields with courage and conviction, and to the relentless pursuit of a secure digital future. This book is dedicated to all the unsung heroes of cybersecurity, who strive to protect the world from the unseen threats lurking in the digital abyss.

Preface

In the ever-evolving landscape of the digital world, where the lines between reality and the virtual realm blur, cybersecurity has become paramount. This book, "Shadows and Shields," invites you on a journey into the heart of this dynamic field, where ethical hacking and defense strategies collide.

As a cybersecurity expert, ethical hacker, and former red teamer, I have witnessed firsthand the intricacies and challenges of safeguarding our digital infrastructure. Through this narrative, I aim to demystify the world of cybersecurity, revealing the techniques and strategies that underpin both the threats and the defenses.

"Shadows and Shields" goes beyond technical details, offering a glimpse into the mind of a red teamer, the thought processes, and the ethical dilemmas encountered in the pursuit of security. It is a testament to the power of knowledge, the importance of ethical hacking, and the critical need to bridge the gap between those who seek to exploit vulnerabilities and those who dedicate themselves to protecting them.

This book is for cybersecurity professionals, ethical hackers, students, and anyone fascinated by the digital world. It is a guide to understanding the complex world of cybersecurity and a call to action to empower ourselves and others to navigate the challenges of a secure digital future.

Introduction

The digital landscape is a battleground, a constant tug-of-war between those who seek to exploit vulnerabilities and those who tirelessly defend against them. This book takes you inside the trenches, offering an intimate look at the world of cybersecurity through the eyes of a seasoned ethical hacker.

Michael Anthony Trevino Jr., the protagonist of our story, is a cybersecurity expert whose journey began under the guidance of the legendary Kevin Mitnick. He learned the art of red teaming, mastering the techniques used by hackers to uncover vulnerabilities and expose weaknesses in systems. However, Michael's passion for cybersecurity extends beyond the realm of offense. He seeks to use his knowledge and skills to protect and defend, to empower individuals and organizations to build a more secure digital world.

"Shadows and Shields" delves into the complexities of ethical hacking, exploring the mindset, skills, and ethical considerations that guide this unique profession. It dissects the creation of custom zero-day exploits, including remote code execution vulnerabilities and zero-click exploits targeting mobile devices, showcasing the power and potential danger of this knowledge.

But beyond the technical intricacies, the book examines the ethical framework that underpins ethical hacking. It delves into the moral dilemmas faced by those operating in the gray areas of cybersecurity, highlighting the importance of integrity and responsibility.

This narrative is more than just a story about hacking; it is a journey into the heart of cybersecurity, exploring the techniques used to defend against evolving threats, the importance of a strong security posture, and the critical need for ongoing vigilance in a world increasingly dependent on digital infrastructure.

Join us as we unravel the secrets of cybersecurity, learn from the experience of a master red teamer, and gain a deeper understanding of the ever-evolving battle between shadows and shields.

Meeting the Mentor

The air crackled with anticipation as Michael Anthony Trevino Jr. found himself standing before a legend. His heart pounded in his chest like a drum solo, a symphony of excitement and nervous energy. This wasn't just any meeting; this was a chance to learn from the master himself, Kevin Mitnick.

Kevin Mitnick, the infamous hacker who had once evaded the FBI for years, had become a renowned cybersecurity expert, author, and speaker. He was a mythical figure in the cybersecurity world, a symbol of both the dark and the light side of the digital realm. Michael, a young and aspiring cybersecurity expert, had been captivated by Mitnick's story since his teenage years. He was mesmerized by Mitnick's audacity, his technical prowess, and his subsequent transformation into a force for good in the cybersecurity landscape.

The meeting was arranged by a mutual friend, a seasoned cybersecurity professional who recognized the potential in both men. Michael had spent years honing his skills, meticulously studying every aspect of cybersecurity, and he was eager to absorb knowledge from the best. He had prepared meticulously, his mind overflowing with questions, anxieties, and a burning desire to prove himself worthy of Mitnick's time.

The meeting took place in a small, unassuming office in the heart of Silicon Valley. It was a far cry from the glamorous headquarters of tech giants, but it held a certain charm, a sense of history etched into its walls. The room was sparsely furnished, with a worn leather armchair facing a desk cluttered with papers, books, and an assortment of electronic gadgets.

As Michael nervously shuffled into the room, Mitnick greeted him with a warm smile that disarmed his apprehension. Mitnick's piercing blue eyes, framed by thick black glasses, seemed to hold a world of knowledge and experience. He had a quiet presence, a calming aura that immediately eased Michael's tension.

"Michael, it's a pleasure to finally meet you," Mitnick said, extending his hand. "I've heard great things about your work."

Michael stammered a thank you, his voice shaking slightly. He had never met anyone who had had such a profound impact on his life. He felt like a child meeting his hero, awestruck by the magnitude of Mitnick's achievements and reputation.

Mitnick motioned for him to sit down, his gaze unwavering. "So, tell me, Michael, what brings you here today?"

Michael cleared his throat, his apprehension fading as he realized that Mitnick was not the intimidating figure he had imagined. Instead, he exuded a genuine interest in Michael's journey and aspirations. "I've always been fascinated by cybersecurity," Michael began, his voice gaining confidence with each word. "And I've always admired your work, Mr. Mitnick. Your stories, your exploits, your transition into a champion for ethical hacking – it's all been incredibly inspiring."

Mitnick chuckled softly, his eyes twinkling with amusement. "Call me Kevin, Michael. And thanks for the kind words. I've always believed that knowledge should be shared, and that the best way to fight bad actors is to educate others about how they operate."

"I want to learn from you, Kevin," Michael declared, his voice brimming with enthusiasm. "I want to understand the hacker's mindset, the art of red teaming, and how to use my skills to protect companies and individuals from cyber threats."

Mitnick leaned back in his chair, studying Michael intently. "You've come to the right place, Michael. I've always said that the best way to defend against something is to understand how it works."

And so, the journey began. Michael found himself immersed in a world of knowledge, wisdom, and real-world insights. Mitnick shared his vast experience, his insights into the intricate world of cybercrime, and the ethical challenges that came with navigating the gray areas of the digital landscape.

"Think like a hacker, Michael," Mitnick would say, his voice calm and measured. "Understand their motivations, their techniques, their tools. Only then can you truly protect against them."

Michael absorbed every word like a sponge, his mind racing with questions and insights. He learned about social engineering, how hackers manipulate human psychology to gain access to sensitive information. He delved into the intricacies of exploit development, crafting custom malware to expose vulnerabilities in software systems. He explored the dark underbelly of the internet, where criminal networks exchanged stolen data and black market tools.

Mitnick guided him through the labyrinthine world of cybersecurity, teaching him the importance of vulnerability research, penetration testing, and responsible disclosure. He stressed the need for a strong ethical compass, emphasizing the importance of using one's skills for good.

"The lines can blur, Michael," Mitnick warned. "The temptation to exploit vulnerabilities for personal gain can be overwhelming. But remember, true power lies in using your knowledge to protect, not to harm."

Michael took Mitnick's words to heart. He saw the power he could wield, not only to identify and exploit vulnerabilities, but also to build secure systems and protect innocent people from harm. It was a responsibility he embraced with fervor, a commitment he made to himself and to the world.

Over time, Michael developed a deep respect for Mitnick's expertise and his unwavering commitment to ethical hacking. He saw in Mitnick a mentor, a guide, and a living embodiment of the values he aspired to embody.

"You're a natural, Michael," Mitnick said one evening, as they reviewed a recent red team operation. "You have a keen eye for detail, a sharp mind, and a willingness to learn. You have the potential to be a truly exceptional cybersecurity professional."

Michael's heart swelled with pride. He knew he still had much to learn, but having Mitnick's recognition and guidance gave him the confidence to push his boundaries, to delve deeper into the complexities of cybersecurity, and to embrace the challenges that lay ahead.

"Thank you, Kevin," Michael replied, his voice filled with gratitude. "I couldn't have asked for a better mentor."

As their time together progressed, Michael realized that Mitnick's influence extended far beyond technical expertise. He was a master of persuasion, a charismatic figure who could inspire and motivate others to action. He taught Michael the importance of communication, collaboration, and the art of storytelling in the world of cybersecurity.

"People need to understand the threats they face, Michael," Mitnick would explain. "You have to be able to tell a compelling story, to paint a picture of the risks, to make them see the importance of security."

Michael started to incorporate Mitnick's teachings into his own approach to cybersecurity. He began to write articles, publish blog posts, and deliver presentations, sharing his knowledge and passion with a wider audience. He realized that he had a gift for storytelling, for explaining complex technical concepts in a way that was engaging and accessible to everyone.

The bond between Michael and Mitnick grew stronger with each passing day. They shared a passion for cybersecurity, a thirst for knowledge, and a deep commitment to protecting the digital world. They forged a friendship built on mutual respect, shared experiences, and a common goal to make the digital world a safer place for everyone.

Their journey together was just beginning, a path that would lead them through the darkest corners of the digital landscape and into the light of a secure and ethical future. Michael was ready to embrace the challenges that lay ahead, armed with the knowledge, skills, and ethical compass that Mitnick had instilled in him. The genesis of a cyber warrior had begun.

First Steps into the Digital Abyss

The smell of burnt popcorn lingered in the air, a stark reminder of the countless hours I spent glued to my computer screen. It was the early 2000s, and the internet was my playground, a boundless realm teeming with hidden pathways and digital treasures. But as I delved deeper, the allure of exploration gave way to a newfound curiosity—a thirst to understand the unseen forces that lurked beneath the surface of this virtual landscape.

It began innocently enough, with a fascination for the intricate workings of software. I'd spend hours dissecting code, piecing together the logic behind seemingly mundane programs. The thrill of unraveling their secrets ignited a spark within me, a yearning to push beyond the limitations of what was known.

One fateful day, I stumbled upon a website dedicated to computer security—a portal to a world I had never imagined. It was there, amidst the cryptic jargon and technical discussions, that I encountered the name Kevin Mitnick.

The mention of his name sent a shiver down my spine. To the world, he was a notorious hacker, a modern-day Robin Hood who had stolen millions of dollars and defied the authorities with his audacious exploits. But to me, he was a legend, a symbol of ingenuity and technical mastery. I was captivated by his story, drawn to the mystique surrounding his ability to penetrate systems with such precision.

As I devoured everything I could find about Mitnick, a desire to learn his craft took root within me. I craved the knowledge, the skill, the understanding that could unlock the secrets he had mastered.

My initial foray into cybersecurity was a haphazard affair, a jumble of trial and error. I devoured tutorials, delved into forums, and experimented with rudimentary hacking tools. Each attempt, each success, and each failure solidified my determination to learn more, to push my boundaries further.

My early experiments were often clumsy and ineffective. I'd try to exploit vulnerabilities, but my attempts were easily thwarted by basic security measures. I was still learning the language of code, the syntax of vulnerabilities, the nuances of system defenses.

I started small, analyzing simple websites, searching for common flaws in their programming. I learned about SQL injection attacks, cross-site scripting vulnerabilities, and the basic principles of network reconnaissance. My arsenal of tools grew alongside my understanding, each new technique adding another layer to my repertoire.

It was through this trial and error process that I began to grasp the fundamentals of cybersecurity. I discovered the power of observation, the importance of critical thinking, and the value of meticulous planning. The thrill of discovery was intoxicating, the knowledge I acquired a precious treasure.

But alongside the excitement came a growing awareness of the potential consequences of my actions. I understood that the skills I was learning could be wielded for good or for ill, that the line between ethical hacking and malicious intent was a thin one.

This realization, coupled with the unwavering influence of Kevin Mitnick's story, led me to a crucial decision. I resolved to dedicate my newfound knowledge to the pursuit of good, to use my skills to protect systems and individuals from the very threats I was learning to create.

It was a path less traveled, one that demanded discipline, dedication, and an unwavering commitment to ethical conduct. The world of cybersecurity was a vast and intricate domain, filled with challenges and opportunities alike. I knew I had only just begun my journey, but I was determined to walk it with purpose, to become a force for good in the digital realm.

One of my early mentors, a seasoned cybersecurity professional named John, became a guiding force in shaping my understanding of ethical hacking. He instilled in me the importance of respecting boundaries, understanding the legal framework, and always acting with integrity. He emphasized that true cybersecurity experts are not simply skilled hackers but also responsible individuals who prioritize ethical behavior and responsible disclosure.

John's wisdom was instrumental in shaping my approach to cybersecurity. I learned to view every challenge as an opportunity for learning and growth, to seek knowledge with a sense of responsibility, and to always prioritize the greater good.

My initial foray into cybersecurity was a chaotic mix of curiosity, experimentation, and a growing understanding of the potential impact of my actions. It was through this tumultuous period that I discovered my calling, my purpose. I was no longer just a curious teenager, but a budding cyber warrior, determined to wield my skills for good and protect the digital world from those who would exploit it. The journey ahead was daunting, but I was ready to embrace the challenges and opportunities that lay before me.

As I delved deeper into the world of cybersecurity, I learned that the digital landscape is constantly evolving, always presenting new challenges and opportunities. The threats we face today are far more sophisticated than those I encountered in my early days, requiring a more nuanced and adaptable approach to security.

The internet, once a playground of discovery and exploration, has become a battlefield of digital warfare, with cyberattacks becoming more frequent and more destructive. The stakes have risen, and the need for skilled and ethical cybersecurity professionals is paramount.

I am proud to be a part of this fight, to use my knowledge and experience to protect individuals and organizations from the growing threats that endanger our digital world. My journey into the digital abyss has been transformative, a relentless pursuit of knowledge and purpose, driven by a desire to make a difference in a world increasingly reliant on technology.

This story is not merely a tale of technical prowess but a testament to the power of determination, ethics, and a passion for safeguarding the digital world. It's a story that underscores the importance of cybersecurity as a critical pillar of modern society, a field where knowledge, skill, and integrity are inextricably intertwined.

Discovering Red Teaming

It was during one of our late-night hacking sessions, fueled by pizza and endless cups of coffee, that Kevin first mentioned the term "red teaming." It was like a whisper in the digital wind, a secret code that unlocked a whole new dimension of cybersecurity.

"Think of it like a war game," Kevin explained, his eyes gleaming with that mischievous spark I had come to admire. "You're not just trying to break into systems, you're trying to think like the enemy. You're simulating an attack, but from the inside out."

The concept fascinated me. It was the art of playing the villain, not just to exploit vulnerabilities but to learn how to strengthen defenses. It was a dance of deception, a carefully choreographed performance designed to expose weaknesses before they could be exploited.

"It's all about putting your skills to the test," Kevin continued, leaning back in his chair. "It's about pushing boundaries, finding the weak points, and then figuring out how to fix them before the real bad guys can exploit them."

Kevin described red teaming as a dynamic process, a constant back-and-forth between the attackers and the defenders. The goal wasn't simply to break in, but to understand the adversary's methods, their motivations, and their tactics. It was like a chess game, with each move revealing a new layer of complexity, a new opportunity for learning.

The idea resonated with me deeply. It was a world where the line between good and evil blurred, where the only way to truly understand the darkness was to embrace it, to become a temporary shadow walker in the digital landscape.

"You have to think like a hacker," Kevin emphasized, his voice taking on a serious tone. "You have to understand their mindset, their motivations, their tools, and their techniques. Only then can you truly build defenses that will stand up to their attacks."

Kevin's lessons were a revelation. They weren't just about code and technical skills; they were about understanding the human element, the psychology of a hacker. It was a deep dive into the world of grey hats and black hats, the shadowy figures lurking in the digital shadows, waiting for their opportunity to strike.

We began by dissecting real-world cyber attacks. I devoured case studies, analyzing the strategies, the tactics, and the tools employed by attackers. Each case was a puzzle, a complex web of interconnected threads that led back to the heart of the attack.

Kevin taught me to break down the attack into its individual components: the initial reconnaissance, the target selection, the penetration techniques, the data exfiltration, and the cover-up. We dissected the social engineering tactics used to gain access, the phishing campaigns designed to trick unsuspecting users, and the malware crafted to steal sensitive information.

It wasn't just about understanding the attack; it was about understanding the attacker's mindset. Why were they targeting this specific company? What were their motivations? What were they hoping to gain?

"Every attack has a story behind it," Kevin said, his eyes twinkling with a knowing smile. "You have to learn to read between the lines, to decipher the silent language of the digital world."

He introduced me to the world of social engineering, where the human element played a crucial role. We studied the psychology of persuasion, the power of manipulation, and the vulnerabilities inherent in human behavior. We learned how hackers could exploit trust, fear, and greed to gain access to sensitive information.

"You have to think like a con artist," Kevin said, his voice taking on a playful tone. "You have to know how to convince people to give you what you want, even if they don't want to give it to you."

The more I learned about red teaming, the more I realized it was about a profound understanding of the human element in cybersecurity. It was about understanding the motivations behind the attacks, the vulnerabilities that hackers exploit, and the ways in which human behavior can be manipulated.

As my red teaming skills grew, so did my sense of responsibility. I wasn't just a hacker anymore; I was a defender, a warrior fighting against the forces of darkness in the digital realm.

But it wasn't just about technology or skills; it was about the ethical implications of what we were doing. The line between ethical hacking and malicious intent was thin, and it was my responsibility to ensure that I was using my powers for good.

Kevin instilled in me the importance of ethical hacking. It wasn't just about exploiting vulnerabilities, it was about using that knowledge to build stronger defenses, to make the digital world a safer place.

"It's about using your skills to protect, not to harm," Kevin emphasized, his voice firm. "You have the power to make a difference, to make the digital world a more secure place for everyone."

Red teaming wasn't just about technical expertise; it was about a deep understanding of the adversary, their tactics, and their motivations. It was about thinking like a hacker, but not to exploit, but to defend.

And as I delved deeper into the world of red teaming, I began to understand the true purpose of this enigmatic art form: to illuminate the shadows, to expose the weaknesses, and to build stronger defenses for a more secure digital future. It was a journey of discovery, a constant exploration of the ever-evolving landscape of cybersecurity.

This was more than just a job; it was a mission, a calling to protect the digital world from the ever-growing threat of cyberattacks. It was a journey into the heart of the digital jungle, a journey where shadows and shields collided, where the battle for digital security was fought, and where the future of the digital world hung in the balance.

It was a journey I was determined to take, a journey that would shape my future as a cybersecurity warrior, a journey guided by the wisdom of Kevin Mitnick, the legendary hacker who taught me the secrets of the digital world and the power of red teaming.

The Art of Ethical Hacking

The world of ethical hacking, shrouded in mystique and often misunderstood, holds a unique allure. It's a realm where curiosity intertwines with a deep understanding of technology, where vulnerabilities are unearthed not to exploit but to strengthen. This is where Michael Anthony Trevino Jr. found his calling, guided by the wisdom of the legendary Kevin Mitnick.

In the early days of his journey, Michael discovered a passion for understanding how systems worked, not just on the surface, but beneath the veneer. He sought to unravel the intricacies of code, to identify the hidden pathways that could be exploited. This fascination led him to the world of red teaming, a practice where ethical hackers simulate real-world attacks to identify weaknesses in a system.

Red teaming, however, is more than just a technical exercise; it's a dance with morality, a delicate balance between exploration and responsibility. Ethical hackers, like Michael, are entrusted with a unique privilege—the ability to peek into the shadows of the digital world, but with the unwavering commitment to use their knowledge for good. They are the guardians of the digital realm, the defenders against the dark forces that lurk in the ether.

The ethical hacker's creed is built on a foundation of integrity and a profound respect for the systems they probe. They understand that their actions have far-reaching consequences, and they operate within a strict ethical framework. Their mission is not to inflict harm but to help organizations bolster their defenses, to make the digital world a safer place for everyone.

The ethical hacker's journey is driven by a profound sense of curiosity. It's the desire to uncover the secrets of the digital world, to understand how systems tick, and to find the hidden vulnerabilities that could be exploited. But this curiosity is tempered by a strong sense of responsibility. Ethical hackers are not merely explorers; they are protectors, guardians of the digital realm.

The art of ethical hacking lies in the intricate dance between technical expertise and ethical awareness. It's a constant push and pull between the allure of discovery and the imperative to safeguard. Every line of code, every vulnerability uncovered, is a delicate balancing act.

Ethical hackers must navigate a complex landscape, where the lines between right and wrong are often blurred. They must be able to discern the intent behind an action, to separate the malicious from the curious, to distinguish between a genuine threat and an innocent oversight. They must be able to anticipate the consequences of their actions, both intended and unintended.

Michael, mentored by Kevin Mitnick, learned to embrace this ethical compass. He understood that his knowledge was a powerful tool, one that could be used for good or for ill. He chose the path of the defender, dedicating himself to using his skills to strengthen the defenses of organizations against the very threats he could create.

One of the defining principles of ethical hacking is transparency. Ethical hackers operate in the open, collaborating with organizations and individuals to improve security. They share their findings and their insights, empowering others to strengthen their defenses. This transparency is vital for building trust and fostering a culture of collaboration within the cybersecurity community.

Ethical hacking is more than just a profession; it's a calling. It's a commitment to safeguarding the digital world, to protecting individuals and organizations from the ever-growing threat of cyberattacks. It's a mission that demands both technical prowess and a deep sense of ethical responsibility.

Michael, driven by this ethical compass, honed his skills, crafting custom zero-day exploits, the most potent weapons in the digital arsenal. He understood the risks inherent in such endeavors, the power he wielded. He was a double-edged sword, capable of both inflicting damage and protecting against it.

The world of ethical hacking is a constant battle against the forces of darkness. It's a battle that demands resilience, creativity, and an unwavering commitment to ethical principles. Ethical hackers are the unsung heroes of the digital age, the defenders of the realm, the guardians of the digital commons.

Their work is often unseen, their efforts often underappreciated, but their impact is profound. They work behind the scenes, identifying vulnerabilities, strengthening defenses, and ensuring the safety of the digital world we all rely on.

Their story is one of dedication, ingenuity, and unwavering commitment to ethics. It's a story of a world where the lines between light and darkness are often blurred, where curiosity and responsibility must walk hand in hand. It's a story of the silent defenders, the guardians of the digital realm, the ethical hackers who stand watch over the digital world.

Ethical hackers are not simply technicians; they are thinkers, strategists, and problem solvers. They operate in a world of constant change, where new threats emerge every day. They must be able to adapt, to learn, and to innovate, always staying one step ahead of the adversaries.

Ethical hacking is a constant learning process. It's a journey of discovery, where every new vulnerability, every new exploit, expands the horizon of knowledge. It's a journey that demands a thirst for knowledge, a relentless pursuit of understanding, and a willingness to push the boundaries of what's possible.

The ethical hacker's journey is not without its challenges. It's a world where the stakes are high, where the consequences of failure can be significant. It's a world where the lines between right and wrong are often blurred, where ethical dilemmas are commonplace.

In the face of these challenges, ethical hackers must maintain their unwavering commitment to ethics. They must be guided by a strong moral compass, by a deep sense of responsibility, and by a commitment to using their knowledge for good. They must remember that their actions have the power to shape the digital world, and they must strive to use that power for the benefit of all.

The ethical hacker's story is a story of courage, ingenuity, and dedication. It's a story of individuals who have chosen to use their skills to protect the digital world, to make it a safer, more secure place for everyone. It's a story that inspires, that challenges, and that reminds us of the power of technology, and the importance of using it responsibly.

Michael Anthony Trevino Jr.'s journey is a testament to the power of ethical hacking. It's a story of a man who chose to use his skills for good, to protect the digital world from the forces of darkness. It's a story that serves as a beacon of hope, a reminder that even in the darkest corners of the digital world, there are those who stand guard, the ethical hackers, the defenders of the realm.

Crafting the Blueprint

Michael's journey into the world of cybersecurity wasn't a linear progression; it was a winding path paved with curiosity, passion, and a relentless pursuit of knowledge. His early fascination with computers and the digital realm quickly blossomed into a deep-seated desire to understand the hidden complexities of the online world. This thirst for knowledge led him to explore the depths of coding, delving into the intricacies of programming languages and software development. It was in these early years, while still in his teens, that Michael stumbled upon a world of hidden vulnerabilities and covert exploits. He was captivated by the idea of pushing the boundaries of conventional security protocols, intrigued by the challenge of uncovering weaknesses in systems designed to be impenetrable. This newfound interest ignited a spark within him, a yearning to delve deeper into the shadowy realm of cybersecurity.

Michael's approach to learning was anything but conventional. He wasn't content with passively absorbing information from textbooks or online courses. Instead, he embraced a hands-on, experiential approach, determined to learn by doing. This meant diving headfirst into the world of hacking, meticulously studying the techniques and strategies employed by those who sought to exploit vulnerabilities. His passion for understanding the "why" behind every attack propelled him to dissect every line of code, every network protocol, and every security measure. He spent countless hours poring over technical documentation, dissecting malware samples, and deciphering the intricate workings of network protocols.

Michael's dedication to mastery was evident in his meticulous approach to skill development. He viewed each new technique, each exploit, and each security measure as a puzzle to be solved, a challenge to be conquered. He approached his learning with a systematic framework, breaking down complex concepts into manageable chunks and meticulously documenting every step of his exploration. He meticulously documented his findings, compiling notes, diagrams, and code snippets into a personal library of knowledge. This methodical approach allowed him to develop a deep understanding of the underlying principles that governed cybersecurity.

Michael's journey into the world of cybersecurity was further propelled by a fateful encounter with a legendary figure – Kevin Mitnick, the infamous hacker turned security consultant. This meeting was a pivotal moment in Michael's life, a turning point that shaped his destiny. Mitnick's unique perspective on cybersecurity, his blend of technical brilliance and ethical conviction, profoundly influenced Michael's own approach to the field. It was Mitnick who introduced Michael to the concept of red teaming, a methodology that involved simulating real-world cyberattacks to identify and exploit vulnerabilities within a company's security infrastructure. This practice, however, wasn't about causing harm or exploiting weaknesses for malicious purposes. It was about exposing vulnerabilities, testing the limits of security measures, and ultimately strengthening a company's defenses.

Mitnick became Michael's mentor, guiding him through the complexities of ethical hacking and red teaming. He instilled in Michael the importance of using his knowledge for good, not for personal gain or malicious intent. Mitnick emphasized the critical role of ethical hackers in safeguarding the digital world, helping organizations to identify and mitigate vulnerabilities before they could be exploited by malicious actors. This emphasis on ethical hacking, on using one's skills for the greater good, deeply resonated with Michael's own values.

Driven by a desire to contribute to a more secure digital world, Michael began to develop a strategic approach to his cybersecurity learning. He recognized that mastering this field required more than just technical expertise; it demanded a comprehensive understanding of the human element, the motivations, and the psychology that underpinned cyberattacks. This realization led him to delve into the psychology of cybersecurity, exploring the mindsets and thought processes of hackers, and the vulnerabilities that they exploited. He studied the techniques used by malicious actors, analyzing their attack vectors, their tactics, and their ultimate goals.

Michael's approach to learning was characterized by a constant cycle of exploration, experimentation, and refinement. He wasn't afraid to fail, to make mistakes, and to learn from them. He viewed each setback as an opportunity to improve, to refine his skills, and to push himself further. He diligently documented his findings, creating a detailed repository of knowledge, a roadmap of his learning journey. This meticulous approach, this unwavering commitment to self-improvement, formed the bedrock of his success in the field of cybersecurity.

Michael's journey into the world of cybersecurity was a testament to the power of passion, perseverance, and a relentless pursuit of knowledge. It was a journey that began with a spark of curiosity and blossomed into a deep-seated commitment to safeguarding the digital world. He didn't just learn about cybersecurity; he lived it, breathed it, and embodied it. His commitment to excellence, his dedication to ethical hacking, and his unwavering drive to build a more secure digital future were the hallmarks of his journey. This journey, however, was just the beginning. Michael's story was far from over. He had much more to learn, many more challenges to overcome, and countless opportunities to contribute to a safer digital landscape. His path, paved with the lessons learned from his mentor, Kevin Mitnick, and fueled by his insatiable curiosity and desire to make a difference, was just starting to unfold.

The Psychology of Cybersecurity

The realm of cybersecurity is a battlefield of minds, a constant game of cat and mouse between those who seek to protect and those who seek to exploit. To navigate this digital landscape effectively, one must understand the psychology of cybersecurity, the very essence of the hacker's mindset. It's not just about technical skills; it's about understanding the motivations, thought processes, and strategies that drive both the defenders and the attackers.

The hacker's mind is a curious thing, a blend of intellectual curiosity, creative problem-solving, and a penchant for pushing boundaries. Imagine a detective, driven not by solving crimes but by unraveling intricate puzzles, seeking out hidden patterns and vulnerabilities. This is the essence of the hacker's mindset: an insatiable thirst for knowledge, a relentless pursuit of understanding the inner workings of systems, and a fascination with uncovering hidden secrets.

Think of it as a form of intellectual exploration, a journey into the heart of digital landscapes, seeking out the weak points, the vulnerabilities, the cracks in the system. This quest for knowledge is not motivated by malicious intent; it's about understanding the mechanics, the logic, and the potential flaws inherent in the digital world.

This inquisitiveness, however, needs to be tempered with a strong sense of ethics. The ethical hacker, unlike the malicious one, operates within a framework of moral responsibility. They use their knowledge and skills for good, working to identify and exploit vulnerabilities in a controlled environment, ultimately to strengthen security and protect systems from real-world threats.

It's a delicate dance, this balance between curiosity and ethics, between exploration and responsibility. The ethical hacker recognizes that their knowledge can be used for both good and ill, and they choose the path of protection, wielding their skills as a shield against the forces that seek to exploit and disrupt.

To truly understand the hacker's mindset, one must delve into their thought processes, their strategies, and their approaches to problem-solving. It's about recognizing the patterns in their behavior, the telltale signs of an attack, and the techniques they employ to gain access and control.

Think of it as a chess game, where every move is calculated, every action carefully considered. Hackers analyze systems, map out vulnerabilities, and craft intricate strategies to achieve their objectives. It's a game of strategy, a test of ingenuity, and a battle of wits.

The ethical hacker, in turn, must become a master of this game, understanding the opponent's moves, predicting their actions, and anticipating their next steps. They must be able to think like a hacker, to see the world through their eyes, to anticipate their tactics and defenses.

This is where the psychology of cybersecurity comes into play. It's not enough to simply understand the technical aspects of security; one must also comprehend the human element, the motivations, the desires, and the vulnerabilities that drive both the attackers and the defenders.

This understanding allows ethical hackers to not only identify weaknesses but also to anticipate potential threats. It helps them build stronger defenses, craft better strategies, and ultimately, create a more secure digital world.

To illustrate this point, let's consider a real-world example. Imagine a hacker targeting a company's network. They might start by researching the company's online presence, gathering information about their employees, their products, and their systems. They might then use social engineering techniques to gain access to the company's internal network, exploiting human vulnerabilities and manipulating their trust.

The ethical hacker, on the other hand, would take a different approach. They might conduct a penetration test, simulating a real-world attack to identify vulnerabilities and weaknesses in the company's security posture. They might then work with the company to implement security measures to mitigate these risks, creating a more secure environment for their data and their operations.

In essence, the ethical hacker becomes a partner in the company's security journey, not an adversary. They are the trusted advisor, the voice of reason, the guardian of the digital realm.

This is the heart of the psychology of cybersecurity: understanding the motivations, the strategies, and the vulnerabilities of both the attackers and the defenders. It's about learning to think like a hacker, to anticipate their moves, and to create a more secure world for all.

Delving Deeper: The Mind of a Hacker

Now, let's delve deeper into the specific cognitive processes that drive hackers. What makes them tick? What fuels their relentless pursuit of knowledge and exploitation?

The hacker's mindset is often driven by a potent cocktail of curiosity, intellectual stimulation, and a desire to challenge the status quo. Think of it as a puzzle: the more complex and intricate the puzzle, the more satisfying the solution. Systems and networks become their intricate puzzles, and each vulnerability, each crack in the armor, represents a challenge to be conquered, a puzzle to be solved.

This drive can manifest in different ways. Some hackers might be driven by a desire to showcase their technical skills, to prove their abilities, and to gain recognition within the hacking community. Others might be motivated by a sense of righteousness, believing that they are exposing vulnerabilities to hold those responsible accountable, or to bring about positive change.

And then there are those who are driven by greed, seeking personal gain through financial exploitation, data theft, or other criminal activities. But even within the realm of malicious hacking, there are different motivations at play. Some hackers might be driven by a desire for power, to control systems, networks, and even individuals. Others might be motivated by a sense of revenge, seeking to inflict harm on those who they perceive as having wronged them.

However, regardless of their motivations, hackers tend to share a common set of cognitive traits:

1. Lateral Thinking: Hackers are masters of lateral thinking. They are able to approach problems from unusual angles, thinking outside the box, and finding unconventional solutions. They can see connections and patterns that others might miss, identifying vulnerabilities that are not immediately apparent.

2. Critical Thinking: Hackers possess a strong sense of critical thinking, questioning assumptions, scrutinizing information, and seeking out underlying truths. They are able to dissect systems, identify inconsistencies, and pinpoint weaknesses.

3. Problem-Solving: Hackers are excellent problem solvers. They can analyze complex situations, break them down into manageable components, and devise creative solutions. They can work through challenges systematically, utilizing logic and reasoning to overcome obstacles.

4. Adaptability: Hackers are highly adaptable. They are able to adjust their strategies and tactics in response to changing circumstances. They are quick to learn new tools and techniques, and they are constantly evolving their methods.

5. Persistence: Hackers are persistent. They are not easily deterred by setbacks or failures. They are willing to spend hours, even days, researching, analyzing, and experimenting until they find a way to exploit a vulnerability. Their persistence is fueled by their curiosity, their drive to succeed, and their determination to achieve their goals.

Understanding the Hacker's Mindset: A Key to Stronger Cybersecurity

By understanding these cognitive traits, we can gain a deeper appreciation for the hacker's mindset. This understanding can be invaluable in building stronger cybersecurity defenses, as it allows us to anticipate their moves, to counter their strategies, and to create more resilient systems.

It's about thinking like a hacker, seeing the world through their eyes, and understanding their motivations, their thought processes, and their techniques. It's about learning to play their game, but on our terms, using our knowledge to protect, not exploit.

The Hacker's Toolkit: Weapons of Choice

Now, let's explore the tools and methodologies that ethical hackers use to identify and exploit vulnerabilities. These tools are not just about technical proficiency, but also about a deep understanding of how systems work, how they can be manipulated, and how to leverage their weaknesses.

1. Network Scanning: Network scanning involves sending probes to target systems to gather information about their open ports, services, and vulnerabilities. Tools like Nmap, Nessus, and OpenVAS are widely used for network scanning, allowing hackers to identify potential attack vectors and entry points.

2. Vulnerability Assessment: Vulnerability assessment involves identifying weaknesses in systems and software. Tools like Metasploit, Burp Suite, and OWASP ZAP are used to analyze systems for known vulnerabilities, allowing hackers to determine which exploits might be effective.

3. Penetration Testing: Penetration testing is a simulated attack on a target system to evaluate its security posture. Ethical hackers use a variety of techniques, including network scanning, vulnerability assessment, and social engineering, to simulate real-world attacks and identify vulnerabilities.

4. Social Engineering: Social engineering involves manipulating people to gain access to sensitive information or systems. Techniques like phishing, pretexting, and baiting are used to exploit human vulnerabilities and gain unauthorized access.

5. Exploit Development: Exploit development involves crafting custom code to take advantage of identified vulnerabilities. This process requires a deep understanding of programming languages, software vulnerabilities, and exploit techniques.

6. Reverse Engineering: Reverse engineering involves analyzing software and hardware to understand its inner workings, often with the goal of identifying vulnerabilities or bypassing security measures.

7. Forensics: Forensic analysis involves investigating digital evidence to uncover the cause of an incident, identify the perpetrator, and recover compromised data.

8. Security Auditing: Security auditing involves reviewing security controls and policies to ensure their effectiveness and compliance with industry standards.

The Hacker's Mindset: A Continuous Evolution

The world of cybersecurity is in constant flux, with new vulnerabilities emerging, new threats evolving, and new technologies being introduced. To stay ahead of the curve, ethical hackers must continuously refine their skills, update their knowledge, and adapt to the changing landscape.

They must embrace a mindset of lifelong learning, constantly seeking out new information, new tools, and new techniques. They must be willing to experiment, to push boundaries, and to challenge the status quo.

The hacker's mindset is not a static concept; it's a dynamic and evolving one, constantly adapting to the ever-changing nature of the digital world. It's a mindset that embraces change, innovation, and a relentless pursuit of knowledge, all in the service of a more secure future.

Inside the Mind of a Hacker

The world of cybersecurity is often depicted as a battleground, a constant tug-of-war between defenders and attackers. But to understand this conflict, we need to delve into the minds of those on the offensive side – the hackers. This chapter delves into the intricate cognitive processes that drive hackers, exploring the motivations, thought patterns, and techniques that define their unique approach to the digital world.

Hackers are not simply malicious individuals seeking to wreak havoc. They are often driven by a potent mix of curiosity, intellectual challenge, and a desire to push the boundaries of technology. Their minds are wired to see patterns, identify vulnerabilities, and exploit weaknesses that others might overlook.

At the heart of a hacker's mindset is an unwavering curiosity. They are driven by an insatiable thirst for knowledge, a constant yearning to understand how systems work, and a burning desire to uncover their hidden secrets. This curiosity isn't limited to technical intricacies; it extends to the social and psychological aspects of security as well. Hackers often study human behavior, exploiting vulnerabilities in social engineering techniques to gain unauthorized access.

This insatiable curiosity fuels a relentless drive for innovation. Hackers are constantly seeking new ways to bypass security measures, developing innovative tools and techniques to achieve their objectives. They are masters of improvisation, adapting and evolving their methods to outwit the ever-changing landscape of security defenses.

The hacker's mind is also a playground of intellectual puzzles. They view cybersecurity as a complex game, a challenge to be solved through ingenuity and determination. This competitive spirit drives them to test their skills, to find creative solutions to overcome obstacles, and to outsmart their opponents. The thrill of discovery, the satisfaction of achieving a breakthrough, is a powerful motivator for many hackers.

However, it is important to acknowledge that not all hackers operate with malicious intent. The world of hacking encompasses a spectrum, with individuals ranging from those who exploit vulnerabilities for personal gain to ethical hackers who utilize their skills to strengthen cybersecurity defenses. Ethical hackers, like myself, use the same knowledge and techniques as malicious actors, but with the explicit purpose of identifying and mitigating vulnerabilities before they can be exploited by those with ill intentions.

Understanding the hacker's mindset is crucial for cybersecurity professionals. By grasping their motivations, thought processes, and techniques, we can develop more effective defenses, anticipate emerging threats, and proactively protect critical systems and data. It is through a deep understanding of the hacker's world that we can truly build a secure digital future.

Let's explore some of the key cognitive characteristics that define a hacker's mindset:

Problem-Solving Focus: Hackers are inherently problem solvers. They approach every security challenge with a determination to find a solution, often thinking outside the box to uncover unconventional methods.

Abstract Thinking: They excel at abstract thinking, able to visualize complex systems and processes, and identify vulnerabilities that others might miss. They possess a strong understanding of logical relationships and can readily translate abstract concepts into practical solutions.

Analytical Thinking: Hackers are keen analysts, meticulously dissecting information, identifying patterns, and drawing logical conclusions. They can sift through vast amounts of data, separating the relevant from the irrelevant, to uncover critical clues.

Lateral Thinking: Hackers embrace lateral thinking, exploring multiple avenues and unconventional approaches to find solutions. They are not bound by conventional methods, often utilizing ingenuity and creativity to bypass established security measures.

Resilience and Determination: The path of a hacker is often fraught with challenges, dead ends, and setbacks. They possess an unwavering resilience, refusing to be discouraged by obstacles and persisting until they find a solution.

Creativity and Innovation: Hackers are driven by a relentless quest for innovation. They are always seeking new ways to approach problems, developing unique tools and techniques to exploit vulnerabilities. They are masters of improvisation, adapting and evolving their methods to stay ahead of the curve.

Social Engineering Savvy: Beyond technical expertise, hackers often possess a keen understanding of human psychology. They recognize that people are the weakest link in any security system, and they exploit this vulnerability through social engineering tactics.

Ethical Compass: While some hackers operate with malicious intent, many others are guided by a strong ethical compass. Ethical hackers, like myself, use their skills to identify and mitigate vulnerabilities, ensuring the safety and security of digital systems and information.

Constant Learning: The world of cybersecurity is constantly evolving, and hackers understand the importance of continuous learning. They stay abreast of new threats, vulnerabilities, and technologies, continuously expanding their knowledge base and refining their skills.

Understanding these cognitive processes provides a valuable framework for both ethical hackers and security professionals. By adopting a similar mindset, defenders can better understand the strategies of attackers, anticipate their moves, and build stronger defenses.

Now let's delve into the real-world application of these cognitive characteristics.

Imagine yourself as a hacker, infiltrating a corporate network.

You begin by conducting reconnaissance, gathering information about the target organization. You analyze their website, social media presence, and public records, looking for clues that might reveal vulnerabilities. Your analytical skills kick in as you sift through this information, searching for patterns and inconsistencies.

You discover a seemingly innocuous blog post by a company employee, mentioning their favorite vacation spot. This seemingly irrelevant detail triggers a spark of curiosity in your mind. You apply your lateral thinking skills, connecting this seemingly random piece of information to potential security weaknesses.

You delve deeper, investigating the employee's online activities and social media presence. You find a photo of the employee's vacation home, clearly visible in the background. This information ignites your creativity, leading you to develop a plan to exploit this vulnerability.

You leverage your technical skills to craft a targeted phishing attack, sending an email that appears to be from a trusted source, enticing the employee to click on a malicious link. The email references the employee's vacation home, subtly leveraging their personal interests to gain their trust.

The employee, unsuspecting of the danger, clicks on the link. In an instant, your malware infiltrates their computer, granting you access to the company's network. Your initial curiosity about a seemingly insignificant detail has led to a successful breach.

This scenario illustrates the interplay between different cognitive processes in the mind of a hacker. It demonstrates how curiosity, analytical thinking, lateral thinking, and social engineering savvy can be combined to achieve a successful attack.

But ethical hackers like myself use these same cognitive processes for good. We analyze the vulnerabilities of systems, not to exploit them, but to identify them and strengthen defenses before malicious actors can take advantage. We employ these skills to help organizations build stronger security postures, mitigating potential threats before they can cause harm.

The world of cybersecurity is an ongoing game of cat and mouse, where defenders and attackers constantly adapt and evolve their strategies. By understanding the cognitive processes that drive hackers, we can better equip ourselves to protect our digital world. The knowledge gained from this insight is not only valuable for security professionals but also empowering for individuals who want to safeguard their own digital lives.

Understanding the Hacker's Mindset - Case Studies

The following case studies highlight the importance of understanding the hacker's mindset in mitigating real-world cyber threats:

Case Study 1: The Stuxnet Attack

The Stuxnet worm, discovered in 2010, was a sophisticated piece of malware specifically designed to sabotage Iran's nuclear program. It targeted Siemens industrial control systems, infiltrating critical infrastructure and disrupting the operation of uranium enrichment centrifuges.

The Stuxnet attack was notable for its complexity and targeted nature. It demonstrated a deep understanding of industrial control systems, requiring not only technical expertise but also meticulous planning and execution. The hackers behind the attack, believed to be linked to the United States and Israel, were able to exploit vulnerabilities in the Siemens software, gaining access to the Iranian nuclear facilities.

Insights from Stuxnet:

The attack highlighted the importance of understanding the intricacies of industrial control systems and the vulnerabilities they might present.

It showcased the growing threat of state-sponsored cyberattacks, demonstrating the potential for sophisticated malware to disrupt critical infrastructure.

It underscored the need for robust security measures in industrial environments, including regular vulnerability assessments and proactive threat mitigation strategies.

Case Study 2: The Target Data Breach

In 2013, Target, a major US retailer, suffered a massive data breach that compromised the personal information of millions of customers. The hackers, later identified as a group known as "Fin7," gained access to Target's network through a third-party vendor, exploiting a vulnerability in HVAC system software.

The Target breach illustrated the interconnectedness of modern supply chains and the potential for breaches to occur through seemingly unrelated vulnerabilities. It highlighted the importance of vendor security assessments and due diligence in ensuring the security of third-party systems connected to an organization's network.

Insights from Target:

The attack emphasized the importance of securing the entire attack surface, including third-party vendors and their systems.

It showcased the vulnerability of retailers and other organizations to data breaches, particularly through the use of malware and other sophisticated hacking techniques.

It underscored the need for robust security monitoring and incident response capabilities to detect and mitigate attacks in a timely manner.

Case Study 3: The Equifax Data Breach

In 2017, Equifax, a credit reporting agency, suffered a major data breach that exposed the sensitive personal information of millions of individuals. The hackers exploited a vulnerability in a widely used Apache Struts web framework, gaining unauthorized access to Equifax's systems.

The Equifax breach exposed the dangers of outdated software and the importance of timely patching and vulnerability management. It also highlighted the significant impact of data breaches on individuals and the need for robust data protection regulations.

Insights from Equifax:

The attack demonstrated the critical importance of timely patching and vulnerability management, especially for widely used software frameworks.
It underscored the need for robust security measures to protect sensitive personal data, including encryption and access control mechanisms.
It highlighted the significant legal and financial consequences of data breaches, emphasizing the importance of proactive security measures to mitigate risks.

Conclusion

These case studies illustrate the diverse range of cyberattacks and the significant impact they can have on individuals, organizations, and governments. Understanding the hacker's mindset, their motivations, and their techniques is crucial for developing effective defenses and mitigating threats.

By adopting a similar approach to problem-solving, analytical thinking, creativity, and resilience, cybersecurity professionals can better anticipate attacker strategies, identify vulnerabilities, and build stronger defenses. The battle against cyber threats is a continuous process, requiring constant vigilance, adaptation, and collaboration between defenders and ethical hackers alike.

Building a Hackers Toolkit

Case Studies in Cyber Intrusion

The study of real-world cyber intrusions offers a captivating glimpse into the minds of hackers, revealing their motivations, tactics, and the intricate interplay of technical prowess and psychological manipulation. By dissecting these incidents, we can gain invaluable insights into the hacker psyche, understand their methods, and develop more effective defense strategies.

The NotPetya Ransomware Attack:

The NotPetya attack, launched in 2017, was a devastating ransomware campaign that targeted businesses worldwide. The attackers exploited a vulnerability in a widely used accounting software, allowing them to spread the malware rapidly through corporate networks. NotPetya's impact was particularly severe, causing billions of dollars in damages to companies across various industries. This attack highlights the importance of prioritizing software security and implementing robust patch management practices.

The Target Data Breach:

In 2013, Target, a major retailer, fell victim to a massive data breach that compromised millions of customer credit card details. The attack was orchestrated through a complex chain of events that began with the theft of credentials from a third-party vendor, allowing the attackers to gain access to Target's systems. This incident underscores the need for strong vendor security policies and comprehensive security audits.

The Sony Pictures Hack:

The 2014 Sony Pictures hack was a high-profile cyberattack that targeted the entertainment giant, resulting in the theft of sensitive data, including confidential emails, unreleased movies, and personal information of employees. The attack was attributed to a group of North Korean hackers who sought to retaliate against Sony for producing a film critical of their government. This incident emphasizes the importance of safeguarding data against state-sponsored cyberattacks, which are becoming increasingly sophisticated.

Common Traits of Hackers

These case studies reveal several common traits among hackers, shedding light on their motivations and methods. Many hackers are driven by a combination of factors, including financial gain, intellectual curiosity, political agendas, and even a desire for notoriety.

Financial Gain:

Financial motivations often drive hackers to target businesses and individuals seeking to exploit vulnerabilities for monetary gain. This includes activities like stealing credit card details, selling access to compromised systems, and demanding ransom payments. The NotPetya attack, for instance, aimed to extract financial gain through the ransomware scheme.

Intellectual Curiosity:

Some hackers are driven by a thirst for knowledge and a desire to push the boundaries of their technical abilities. They may be motivated to uncover and exploit security flaws for personal satisfaction or to showcase their skills. This curiosity can lead them to explore vulnerabilities in software, networks, and even hardware, pushing the limits of digital security.

Political Agendas:

Political motivations can also play a significant role in cyber intrusions, as demonstrated by the Sony Pictures hack. Hackers with political objectives may seek to disrupt critical infrastructure, manipulate public opinion, or inflict damage on adversaries.

Notoriety:

The pursuit of notoriety and recognition can also fuel hacking activities. Hackers seeking fame may engage in high-profile cyberattacks to attract attention and gain recognition within the hacking community. This can be achieved through various means, such as breaching high-profile websites, exposing sensitive information, or launching distributed denial-of-service (DDoS) attacks.

Understanding Hacker Techniques

In addition to understanding their motivations, analyzing cyber intrusions allows us to gain insights into the techniques hackers employ.

Social Engineering:

Social engineering is a powerful tool that hackers use to manipulate individuals into compromising their security. This technique relies on psychological manipulation and deception, often exploiting human trust and gullibility. Examples include phishing emails that trick victims into revealing confidential information or pretexting calls that persuade targets to divulge sensitive details.

Exploiting Vulnerabilities:

Hackers frequently exploit software and hardware vulnerabilities to gain unauthorized access to systems. These vulnerabilities can arise from programming errors, design flaws, or outdated software. Once identified, hackers can develop exploits to exploit these weaknesses and gain control of vulnerable systems.

Malware Distribution:

Malware, such as viruses, worms, trojans, and ransomware, plays a crucial role in many cyberattacks. Hackers use various methods to distribute malware, including email attachments, malicious websites, compromised software, and even USB drives. Once installed on a system, malware can steal data, disrupt operations, and even take control of devices.

The Human Element:

While technical skills are essential for hacking, the human element plays a critical role in many cyberattacks. Hackers often rely on social engineering techniques to manipulate individuals into granting them access to systems or divulging sensitive information. Additionally, human error can create vulnerabilities that hackers can exploit, such as failing to update software or using weak passwords.

Conclusion

Analyzing case studies in cyber intrusion provides a valuable window into the minds of hackers, shedding light on their motivations, techniques, and the vulnerabilities they target. Understanding these insights is essential for building robust cybersecurity defenses, mitigating threats, and protecting individuals and organizations from the ever-evolving cyber landscape. By recognizing the common traits of hackers, the techniques they employ, and the crucial role of the human element, we can develop proactive security strategies to counter these threats and build a safer digital world.

Beyond the Case Studies:

While these real-world examples provide valuable lessons, the evolving nature of cyber threats necessitates continuous learning and adaptation. New technologies, emerging vulnerabilities, and innovative hacking techniques constantly emerge, demanding a dynamic and proactive approach to cybersecurity.

The Need for Proactive Defense:

Rather than simply reacting to attacks, organizations must adopt a proactive cybersecurity posture. This involves implementing comprehensive security measures, regularly conducting vulnerability assessments, and actively seeking to identify and mitigate threats before they can exploit vulnerabilities.

The Role of Ethical Hackers:

Ethical hackers, also known as penetration testers or red teamers, play a crucial role in bolstering cybersecurity defenses. They utilize their technical expertise and knowledge of hacker tactics to simulate attacks, uncover vulnerabilities, and help organizations strengthen their security posture. By conducting ethical hacking assessments, organizations can identify and address potential weaknesses before malicious actors can exploit them.

Beyond Technical Skills:

Effective cybersecurity professionals need more than just technical expertise. They must also possess critical thinking skills, analytical abilities, and a strong understanding of human behavior to effectively counter sophisticated cyber threats. This includes recognizing social engineering tactics, understanding the motivations of attackers, and recognizing the potential for human error in security practices.

A Collaborative Approach:

The battle against cybercrime requires a collaborative approach involving governments, organizations, and individuals. Sharing threat intelligence, coordinating defense strategies, and promoting best practices can help organizations stay ahead of emerging threats and build a more resilient cyber ecosystem.

Investing in Security Awareness:

Educating individuals about cybersecurity best practices and common threats is crucial for building a strong defense against cybercrime. This includes raising awareness about phishing attacks, promoting the use of strong passwords, and emphasizing the importance of regularly updating software.

The Ongoing Evolution of Cybersecurity:

Cybersecurity is a constantly evolving field, with new technologies, threats, and vulnerabilities emerging at an alarming rate. Staying informed about the latest trends, techniques, and best practices is essential for staying ahead of the curve and protecting against emerging threats.

The Future of Cybersecurity:

As technology continues to advance, the cyber landscape will become increasingly complex and dynamic. The use of artificial intelligence (AI), machine learning (ML), and automation in cyberattacks and defenses will reshape the cybersecurity landscape. Organizations and individuals must adapt to these evolving threats by embracing innovative security solutions and staying abreast of emerging technologies.

Conclusion:

By analyzing real-world cyber intrusions, understanding the motivations and techniques of hackers, and embracing a proactive approach to cybersecurity, we can build a safer digital world. The journey towards a secure digital future requires continuous learning, collaboration, and a commitment to safeguarding our online world from the ever-present threat of cybercrime.

Balancing Curiosity and Ethics

The hacker's mindset is often shrouded in mystery, a blend of curiosity, technical prowess, and a sometimes-questionable ethical compass. It's a world where the boundaries between good and bad are often blurred, where the thrill of discovery can sometimes overshadow the potential consequences of one's actions.

Michael, having walked the path of both red teamer and ethical hacker, understood this duality intimately. He had spent years immersing himself in the intricate workings of computer systems, learning to exploit vulnerabilities that others might miss. But as he honed his skills, he also grappled with the ethical implications of his knowledge.

"Curiosity is the engine of discovery," Michael would often say, "but it's a powerful engine that needs to be steered with care." His mentor, Kevin Mitnick, had instilled in him a deep respect for the ethical considerations inherent in the world of cybersecurity.

The line between legitimate exploration and malicious intent is a thin one. For some, the allure of exploiting vulnerabilities can lead down a dark path. They may seek personal gain, engage in cybercrime, or even become instruments of state-sponsored hacking. Others, driven by a thirst for knowledge and a desire to improve cybersecurity, channel their curiosity into ethical hacking, working to identify vulnerabilities and help organizations strengthen their defenses.

Michael's journey exemplified this ethical dilemma. He found himself drawn to the challenges of penetration testing, the thrill of unraveling complex security systems, and the satisfaction of uncovering weaknesses. But he also recognized the responsibility that came with this knowledge. He understood that his skills could be misused, and he was determined to use them for good.

One of the most compelling aspects of Michael's journey was his ability to balance curiosity and ethical boundaries. He wasn't afraid to delve into the darkest corners of the digital underworld, but he always maintained a clear moral compass. He believed that by understanding the techniques used by malicious actors, he could better equip organizations to defend against them.

He often reminded his colleagues, "You can't effectively defend against something if you don't understand how it works." This principle guided his approach to red teaming. He would meticulously analyze the systems he was tasked with testing, identifying weaknesses and exploiting them, but always with the ultimate goal of improving security.

This approach, however, was not without its challenges. Michael found himself wrestling with ethical dilemmas, questioning the limits of his own curiosity. He had to constantly remind himself of the potential consequences of his actions, even if they were technically legal and ethically justified. He would spend countless hours debating the fine points of ethical hacking, grappling with the question of when the line between curiosity and malice was crossed.

One particularly challenging case involved a large financial institution. Michael had been hired to conduct a red team assessment, and during his investigation, he stumbled upon a major vulnerability that could have allowed a malicious actor to steal millions of dollars. He debated with himself for days, weighing the ethical implications of reporting the vulnerability versus exploiting it for his assessment.

He knew that disclosing the vulnerability would potentially expose the financial institution to a real-world threat, but he also knew that exploiting it would be a violation of the trust placed in him. Ultimately, he decided to report the vulnerability, choosing to prioritize the safety and security of the institution over the potential success of his assessment.

This decision reflected Michael's commitment to ethical hacking. He understood that true cybersecurity expertise lies not only in the ability to exploit vulnerabilities but also in the integrity and responsibility to use that knowledge for the greater good.

"It's not about the thrill of the hack," Michael would say, "it's about making the world a safer place."

His dedication to ethical hacking extended beyond his professional work. He became an advocate for cybersecurity education, inspiring the next generation of defenders to embrace the challenges and responsibilities of the field. He believed that by sharing his knowledge and experience, he could help build a more secure digital world for everyone.

"We need more ethical hackers, not more malicious actors," he often stressed, "because the fight for cybersecurity is a fight for the future of our world."

As Michael's career progressed, he continued to push the boundaries of cybersecurity expertise, always striving to stay ahead of the evolving landscape of digital threats. He recognized that the world of cybersecurity was a constant game of cat and mouse, with hackers and defenders constantly vying for the upper hand.

But he also recognized that the key to winning this game was not just about technical prowess, but about ethics and responsibility. The true measure of a cybersecurity professional, he believed, was not just in their ability to exploit vulnerabilities but in their commitment to using their knowledge to protect the digital world.

This was the legacy Michael sought to leave behind, a legacy of ethical hacking, a legacy of safeguarding the digital world, and a legacy of inspiring others to join the fight for a secure future.

Understanding ZeroDay Vulnerabilities

Imagine a world where the very foundation of our digital lives is constantly under attack. This isn't a dystopian sci-fi novel; it's the reality of modern cybersecurity. In this world, vulnerabilities lurk in the shadows, waiting to be exploited, and one of the most potent weapons in this invisible war is the zero-day exploit.

Zero-day vulnerabilities are like hidden cracks in the walls of our digital fortresses. These flaws, unknown to developers and security experts, offer hackers a backdoor into our systems, giving them unfettered access to our sensitive data and critical infrastructure. The term "zero-day" stems from the fact that these vulnerabilities are discovered just days or even hours before they are publicly disclosed, leaving little time to patch and defend against them.

Think of it like this: imagine a newly released software program with a secret flaw. The creators, blissfully unaware, roll out the program to millions of users. But in the dark corners of the internet, a group of hackers has already discovered the weakness. They've reverse-engineered the software, pinpointing the flaw that could potentially grant them control of every device running the program. This is the essence of a zero-day vulnerability.

The impact of zero-day exploits can be devastating. Imagine a hacker taking control of a power grid, disrupting energy supplies for millions. Or picture a malicious actor compromising a bank's systems, stealing billions of dollars. These scenarios, unfortunately, are not hypothetical. In recent years, high-profile attacks exploiting zero-day vulnerabilities have made headlines, demonstrating the real-world danger they pose.

The infamous NotPetya ransomware attack of 2017, for instance, exploited a previously unknown vulnerability in Microsoft's Windows operating system, crippling businesses and institutions worldwide. This attack, attributed to Russian-linked hackers, spread like wildfire, infecting thousands of computers and causing billions of dollars in damages.

Another alarming example is the infamous Stuxnet worm, which targeted Iran's nuclear program in 2010. Developed by the United States and Israel, Stuxnet was a highly sophisticated piece of malware designed to sabotage Iran's nuclear centrifuges. This attack exploited a previously unknown vulnerability in Siemens industrial control systems, demonstrating the potential for zero-day exploits to wreak havoc on critical infrastructure.

The allure of zero-day exploits for hackers lies in their ability to bypass traditional security measures. Unlike known vulnerabilities, which are often patched quickly, zero-day exploits offer a window of opportunity before defenses are strengthened. Hackers can exploit these vulnerabilities before they are even identified, making them highly effective in gaining unauthorized access and executing their malicious plans.

However, it's crucial to understand that not all exploits are created equal. Some are more potent than others, capable of wreaking havoc on a grand scale. These are the zero-click exploits, the ultimate weapon in the hacker's arsenal.

Zero-click exploits, as their name suggests, require no user interaction whatsoever. Imagine receiving a seemingly harmless email or text message. Unbeknownst to you, this message carries a malicious payload, silently exploiting a vulnerability in your device. This payload could be a virus, a ransomware attack, or even a backdoor that gives the hacker complete control over your device, all without you ever clicking a single button.

These exploits are particularly insidious because they exploit fundamental flaws in the core operating systems of our devices, such as iOS and Android. The ability to remotely compromise devices without any user intervention makes them extremely dangerous, as they can be used to steal sensitive information, install malware, or even launch attacks on other systems.

The development of zero-click exploits is a complex and sophisticated process. Imagine a group of skilled hackers, armed with advanced tools and a deep understanding of software vulnerabilities. They spend countless hours dissecting the inner workings of operating systems, meticulously searching for flaws. This process is akin to meticulously searching for a hidden needle in a massive haystack, requiring incredible skill and patience.

Once a vulnerability is found, the hackers must craft a custom exploit to leverage it. This involves exploiting the weakness, writing code that bypasses security measures, and ultimately gaining control over the targeted device. This process requires not only technical prowess but also a keen understanding of the target's software and the intricate workings of the underlying operating system.

The development of zero-day exploits has sparked a fierce arms race between hackers and security researchers. As hackers continue to develop increasingly sophisticated exploits, security researchers work tirelessly to identify and patch vulnerabilities before they can be exploited. This cat-and-mouse game plays out in the shadows of the internet, with each side constantly evolving their techniques to stay ahead of the other.

The battle against zero-day exploits is a relentless and evolving struggle. It's a race against time, a constant struggle to anticipate the next threat and strengthen our defenses. But there are strategies to mitigate the impact of these vulnerabilities and protect ourselves from the ever-present threat.

One crucial step is to stay vigilant and constantly update our software and operating systems. Security patches released by software developers often address known vulnerabilities, making it harder for hackers to exploit them. By keeping our systems up-to-date, we can reduce the risk of falling victim to zero-day exploits.

Another crucial strategy is to implement a layered security approach. This means using a combination of different security measures to create a multi-layered defense that makes it harder for hackers to penetrate. This can include firewalls, intrusion detection systems, antivirus software, and other security tools.

In addition to these technical measures, we must also cultivate a culture of cybersecurity awareness. Individuals, businesses, and government agencies must understand the risks posed by zero-day exploits and take proactive steps to protect themselves. This includes being wary of suspicious emails and messages, being cautious about clicking on unknown links, and regularly reviewing security settings on devices and networks.

The fight against zero-day exploits is a continuous struggle, a battle that demands constant vigilance, innovation, and collaboration. As the world of cybersecurity evolves, so too must our defenses. We must remain one step ahead, adapting to the ever-changing landscape of threats and exploiting the tools and knowledge at our disposal to safeguard our digital world.

The story of zero-day exploits is one of innovation, cunning, and the constant struggle to stay ahead of the curve. It is a story that unfolds in the hidden recesses of the digital world, a realm where the lines between good and evil blur and the stakes are constantly rising. It is a story that reminds us that our digital lives are as vulnerable as they are interconnected, and that the fight for cybersecurity is a battle worth fighting.

Crafting Custom Exploits

The thrill of the hunt, the adrenaline rush of discovery, and the satisfaction of outsmarting the enemy—these are the elements that fueled Michael's passion for zero-day exploits. In the realm of cybersecurity, zero-day vulnerabilities were the ultimate challenge, the hidden cracks in the digital armor that could be exploited before anyone even knew they existed.

Imagine a lock, a seemingly impenetrable barrier protecting a valuable vault. Now imagine a key, a unique and unknown key that could unlock this vault before anyone had the chance to secure it. That's what zero-day vulnerabilities represented—a key that existed in the shadows, a key that could open the door to sensitive data, critical systems, or even entire organizations.

Michael's journey into the world of zero-day exploits began with a deep understanding of how software was built. From his early days with Kevin Mitnick, he had learned to dissect applications, analyze their code, and identify weaknesses. But with zero-day vulnerabilities, there were no known weaknesses, no documented flaws to exploit. It was a game of exploration, a search for the unknown, a quest to find the hidden cracks in the digital fabric.

"It's like being a detective," Michael would often say, "but instead of looking for clues in a crime scene, you're looking for vulnerabilities in a piece of software."

His approach was methodical and meticulous. He would start by examining the architecture of a system, understanding how its different components interacted and how information flowed within it. He would then dive deep into the code, studying its structure, analyzing its logic, and searching for any inconsistencies or flaws.

The process of crafting custom exploits for zero-day vulnerabilities was an intricate dance between technical skills, creative thinking, and a touch of luck. It wasn't about brute force or random attacks; it was about strategic thinking, meticulous planning, and an in-depth understanding of the target.

"You're not just looking for a vulnerability," Michael explained, "you're looking for a vulnerability that you can exploit, a vulnerability that you can turn into a weapon."

The first step in crafting a custom exploit was identification —finding that elusive crack in the system's armor. This often involved reverse engineering the software, dissecting it layer by layer, and scrutinizing its every line of code. Michael would use a combination of tools and techniques, including debuggers, disassemblers, and fuzzing tools, to probe the system and uncover its hidden secrets.

Once a potential vulnerability was discovered, the next step was verification—confirming that it was indeed a real weakness and not just a harmless glitch. This involved testing the vulnerability with carefully crafted payloads, designed to trigger specific actions or behaviors within the system.

"It's like playing chess," Michael explained, "You have to anticipate the system's response to your moves, and adjust your strategy accordingly."

If the verification process confirmed the vulnerability, the next step was exploitation—turning the weakness into a weapon. This involved crafting a piece of code, an exploit, specifically designed to take advantage of the vulnerability and achieve a desired outcome.

Exploits could vary in complexity, ranging from simple code snippets to sophisticated multi-step attacks. Some exploits would simply crash the system, disrupting its functionality, while others would allow the attacker to gain control of the system, execute arbitrary code, or steal sensitive data.

"It's a delicate dance," Michael would say, "You have to be precise, you have to be creative, and you have to understand the system you're targeting."

One of the most common types of zero-day exploits was remote code execution (RCE), a technique that allowed an attacker to execute arbitrary code on a remote system. This could be achieved by exploiting vulnerabilities in web applications, network services, or operating systems.

Imagine a website with a form that allows users to upload files. If the website's code doesn't properly validate the uploaded files, an attacker could upload a malicious file that would execute code on the website's server. This could give the attacker control of the server, allowing them to steal data, launch further attacks, or even take over the entire website.

Michael had developed several custom RCE exploits over the years, targeting various web applications and network services. He had learned to exploit vulnerabilities in web servers, databases, and even network protocols, using his knowledge of code, security protocols, and system architecture to craft intricate and effective exploits.

"The key is to understand the system's weaknesses," Michael explained, "and to use those weaknesses to your advantage."

But exploiting vulnerabilities was only one part of the equation. The other part was about timing and discretion.

"The best exploits are the ones that go unnoticed," Michael would say, "The ones that strike silently and leave no trace."

He understood that the success of any exploit depended on its ability to remain undetected. He had learned to craft exploits that could bypass security measures, evade detection by antivirus software, and conceal their actions from system administrators.

He would meticulously analyze the system's defense mechanisms, identify potential detection points, and craft his exploits to avoid triggering alarms or leaving behind any incriminating evidence.

"It's a game of cat and mouse," Michael explained, "You have to stay one step ahead of the defenders."

The world of zero-day exploits was a constantly evolving landscape. New vulnerabilities were discovered every day, and new exploits were being developed at an alarming rate. Michael knew that staying ahead of the curve required constant learning, continuous research, and an insatiable curiosity.

He would spend hours researching the latest software releases, analyzing security updates, and attending conferences and workshops to stay informed about the latest trends in cybersecurity. He would constantly test his skills against new challenges, pushing his limits and expanding his knowledge base.

"It's a never-ending pursuit," Michael would say, "But that's what makes it so exciting."

Beyond technical skills, Michael understood the importance of ethical considerations in the world of zero-day exploits. He recognized that his knowledge could be used for good or for evil, and he was determined to use it for the benefit of society.

He believed that ethical hackers played a vital role in protecting the digital world, by identifying vulnerabilities, informing developers about them, and helping companies build stronger security defenses.

"It's about responsibility," Michael would say, "It's about using your skills to make the world a safer place."

His commitment to ethical hacking led him to share his knowledge with others, to train new generations of cybersecurity professionals, and to advocate for a culture of responsible cybersecurity practices.

"We can't just sit back and wait for the bad guys to strike," Michael explained, "We need to be proactive, we need to be prepared, and we need to work together to protect the digital world."

Michael's journey into the world of zero-day exploits was a testament to his dedication to cybersecurity, his relentless pursuit of knowledge, and his unwavering commitment to protecting the digital world. He had mastered the art of finding the hidden cracks in the system's armor, and he had used his skills to build stronger defenses, empowering companies and individuals to navigate the ever-evolving landscape of cyber threats. His story served as a reminder that in the digital age, the battle for security was a continuous one, a game of strategy, innovation, and unwavering ethical commitment.

Remote Code Execution Exploits

Targeting Mobile Platforms

The world of mobile devices is an exciting landscape for both ethical hackers and security researchers, offering a diverse range of vulnerabilities to explore. In the realm of zero-day exploits, mobile platforms like iOS and Android present unique challenges and opportunities. These platforms are complex ecosystems, constantly evolving with new software updates, security patches, and user interactions. This complexity creates a dynamic environment where vulnerabilities can emerge, vanish, and reappear, making the hunt for zero-day exploits both exhilarating and daunting.

One of the most insidious types of mobile exploits is the zero-click exploit. This type of attack leverages a vulnerability that allows an attacker to compromise a device without any user interaction. The victim simply needs to be within range of the attack, and the malicious payload can be delivered through various means, including SMS messages, MMS messages, or even Wi-Fi networks.

Zero-click exploits are particularly dangerous because they bypass the usual security measures that users rely on, such as screen locks, passwords, and antivirus software. The exploit triggers automatically, often exploiting a flaw in the operating system itself or in a popular application.

To illustrate the potential impact of zero-click exploits, imagine a scenario where a malicious actor targets a high-profile individual, like a CEO or a government official. The attacker crafts a zero-click exploit specifically designed for their device, exploiting a previously unknown vulnerability in a commonly used app. The exploit could deliver a malware payload that grants the attacker complete control over the device, enabling them to steal sensitive data, monitor communications, or even take complete control of the victim's online accounts.

Let's delve into the complexities of zero-click exploits on both iOS and Android platforms.

iOS Exploitation:

iOS, Apple's mobile operating system, is renowned for its security focus. However, despite Apple's best efforts, iOS devices are not immune to zero-day exploits. In recent years, security researchers have uncovered several vulnerabilities that allow attackers to gain unauthorized access to iOS devices.

One example is the "Pegasus" spyware, a sophisticated tool developed by the Israeli company NSO Group. Pegasus exploited a vulnerability in iOS that allowed attackers to remotely install malware on targeted devices, enabling them to intercept messages, record calls, and steal sensitive data.

The Pegasus case highlighted a critical vulnerability in iOS and raised serious concerns about the potential for zero-click exploits to compromise even the most secure devices. Apple responded swiftly, patching the vulnerability and issuing security updates to affected devices. However, this incident demonstrated that the race between attackers and defenders is a constant battle, and new vulnerabilities are always emerging.

Android Exploitation:

Android, Google's mobile operating system, is the most widely used mobile operating system globally. Its open-source nature and the vast number of Android devices make it a tempting target for attackers.

Zero-click exploits on Android devices are a significant concern due to the fragmented nature of the Android ecosystem. With a diverse range of manufacturers, each with its own software customizations, it's challenging to maintain a consistent level of security across all Android devices.

One notorious example of an Android zero-click exploit is the "Stagefright" vulnerability. This vulnerability affected multiple versions of Android and allowed attackers to exploit a flaw in the Android media framework to gain remote code execution capabilities. The vulnerability was so severe that attackers could deliver malware simply by sending a malicious MMS message to the targeted device.

The Stagefright exploit highlighted the critical need for developers and manufacturers to prioritize security and address vulnerabilities promptly. Google responded by releasing security patches to address the Stagefright vulnerability, and many manufacturers followed suit. However, the incident emphasized the challenge of maintaining a high level of security across the vast Android ecosystem.

The Art of Zero-Click Exploitation:

Developing zero-click exploits requires a deep understanding of the underlying operating system and its vulnerabilities. Ethical hackers and security researchers use a variety of techniques to discover and exploit these vulnerabilities.

One common technique is reverse engineering, where researchers deconstruct the operating system or software to identify potential weaknesses. They analyze the code, looking for flaws in the design, implementation, or logic.

Another approach involves fuzzing, where researchers use automated tools to generate random data and input it into the target software or operating system. This approach aims to crash the system or trigger unexpected behavior, revealing vulnerabilities that might otherwise go unnoticed.

Once a vulnerability is identified, researchers must craft a custom exploit to take advantage of it. This process requires a combination of technical skills, creativity, and a thorough understanding of the target platform. The exploit must be carefully designed to bypass the device's security measures and deliver the desired payload.

The Role of Mobile Application Security:

The security of mobile applications is crucial in preventing zero-click exploits. Mobile applications often access sensitive data and can serve as a gateway for attackers to infiltrate devices.

Ethical hackers play a crucial role in assessing the security of mobile applications. They conduct security audits to identify vulnerabilities that could be exploited by malicious actors. These audits involve rigorous testing of the application's code, functionality, and data handling practices.

Security researchers often use specialized tools and techniques to uncover vulnerabilities in mobile applications, including static code analysis, dynamic code analysis, and penetration testing. They also look for common vulnerabilities, such as SQL injection, cross-site scripting, and insecure data storage practices.

Defending Against Zero-Click Exploits:

Defending against zero-click exploits requires a multifaceted approach. Here are some key steps that individuals and organizations can take:

Keeping Devices Updated: Regularly update your device's operating system and applications to the latest security patches. These updates often address known vulnerabilities that could be exploited by attackers.

Using Strong Passwords: Use strong, unique passwords for all your accounts. This helps prevent attackers from gaining access to your devices even if they exploit a vulnerability.

Enabling Two-Factor Authentication: Two-factor authentication adds an extra layer of security by requiring you to provide a code from your phone or other device in addition to your password. This makes it significantly harder for attackers to gain access to your accounts.

Being Cautious of Suspicious Links and Attachments: Do not click on suspicious links or open attachments from unknown senders. These could contain malicious payloads that can compromise your device.

Using Antivirus Software: Install and use a reputable antivirus software on your mobile device. Antivirus software can help detect and remove malware that could be installed through zero-click exploits.

Understanding the Risks of Public Wi-Fi: Be cautious when using public Wi-Fi networks, as they are more vulnerable to attackers. Use a virtual private network (VPN) to encrypt your internet traffic and protect your data.

The Future of Mobile Security:

The battle against zero-click exploits is an ongoing one. Attackers are constantly evolving their techniques, and new vulnerabilities are constantly emerging. To stay ahead of the curve, it's essential to continue investing in security research and development.

One area of focus is the development of more robust security measures for mobile devices. This includes implementing hardware-based security features, such as secure enclaves, and improving the security of the operating systems themselves.

Another critical area is the adoption of new technologies, such as blockchain and decentralized identity systems, to enhance security and privacy. These technologies offer the potential to create a more secure and resilient mobile ecosystem.

Ethical hackers and security researchers play a crucial role in shaping the future of mobile security. By identifying vulnerabilities and developing solutions, they help ensure that mobile devices remain secure and reliable for users worldwide.

Conclusion:

Zero-click exploits pose a significant threat to the security of mobile devices. They can allow attackers to compromise devices without user interaction, enabling them to steal data, monitor communications, and even take complete control of the device. By understanding the complexities of zero-click exploits and implementing robust security measures, we can mitigate the risks and protect our devices from these insidious attacks. The future of mobile security depends on ongoing vigilance, innovation, and collaboration between security professionals, developers, and users.

Mitigating ZeroDay Threats

The discovery of a zero-day vulnerability is a significant event in the cybersecurity world, and it requires immediate action to mitigate its potential impact. The ability to exploit a vulnerability before a patch is available can grant attackers a significant advantage, allowing them to compromise systems, steal sensitive data, or disrupt operations.

The journey to mitigate zero-day threats starts with proactive measures to minimize their impact. One crucial aspect is implementing **robust security practices** that create a layered defense against both known and unknown vulnerabilities. This includes:

Software Patching: Regularly patching software vulnerabilities is the first line of defense against zero-day exploits. This involves updating operating systems, applications, and security software promptly with the latest patches released by vendors. By keeping systems up to date, organizations can close known vulnerabilities, making it harder for attackers to exploit them.

Network Segmentation: Dividing a network into smaller, isolated segments can limit the spread of an exploit if it is successful. This approach restricts access to critical systems and data, making it more difficult for attackers to move laterally across the network and compromise sensitive information.

Security Information and Event Management (SIEM): SIEM systems play a vital role in detecting suspicious activities, including potential zero-day exploit attempts. By analyzing logs and security events from multiple sources, SIEM tools can identify anomalies and flag potential threats.

Endpoint Security: Protecting individual computers and devices is essential in combating zero-day threats. Endpoint security solutions can provide real-time threat detection, malware prevention, and data loss prevention, all of which are crucial for mitigating zero-day vulnerabilities.

Data Loss Prevention (DLP): DLP solutions help prevent sensitive data from leaving the organization's network, even if an exploit grants access. DLP systems monitor data flow, identify confidential information, and block unauthorized attempts to transfer or copy sensitive data.

Beyond these proactive measures, **reactive strategies** are crucial for containing the damage if a zero-day exploit is successful. This involves:

Incident Response Plans: Organizations must have well-defined incident response plans to address security incidents, including those resulting from zero-day exploits. These plans should outline the steps for detecting, analyzing, containing, and recovering from a security breach.

Threat Intelligence: Staying informed about the latest zero-day threats and exploits is vital for proactive defense. By accessing threat intelligence feeds, organizations can gain insights into emerging vulnerabilities, attacker tactics, and potential attack vectors.

Vulnerability Management: Continuously scanning for vulnerabilities and prioritizing their remediation is essential to prevent zero-day exploits. Vulnerability management programs can identify potential weaknesses, assess their severity, and prioritize patching or mitigation efforts.

Sandboxing: Isolating suspicious files or code in a sandbox environment before execution can prevent the spread of malware and protect systems from malicious attacks. Sandboxes provide a controlled environment to analyze potentially harmful software without affecting the production environment.

In addition to these strategies, **collaboration and information sharing** are crucial for mitigating zero-day threats. Organizations can benefit from sharing threat intelligence with each other, industry partners, and cybersecurity research groups. This collective effort can help identify and address vulnerabilities more quickly and effectively.

While the threat of zero-day exploits remains a significant challenge, the advancements in **artificial intelligence (AI) and machine learning (ML)** offer promising solutions. AI-powered security solutions can analyze vast amounts of data, detect anomalies, and identify suspicious activities, enhancing the capabilities of traditional security tools. AI can also assist in identifying zero-day vulnerabilities by analyzing code and predicting potential attack vectors.

The journey to mitigate zero-day threats is an ongoing effort, requiring a combination of proactive and reactive strategies, robust security practices, and constant vigilance. By embracing these principles, organizations can build a stronger defense against the ever-evolving landscape of cybersecurity threats.

Case Study: The Heartbleed Vulnerability

In 2014, the Heartbleed vulnerability, a critical zero-day exploit affecting the OpenSSL encryption library, sent shockwaves through the cybersecurity community. The vulnerability allowed attackers to steal sensitive data, such as usernames, passwords, and credit card details, from millions of websites and services relying on OpenSSL.

The impact of Heartbleed highlighted the importance of proactive patching and vulnerability management. While

OpenSSL developers released a patch for the vulnerability within days of its discovery, many organizations were slow to apply the patch, leaving their systems exposed for weeks. This delay allowed attackers to exploit the vulnerability and steal sensitive data on a massive scale.

The Heartbleed incident demonstrated the critical need for organizations to:

Implement robust vulnerability management programs to identify and prioritize patching efforts.
Stay informed about emerging threats and vulnerabilities through threat intelligence feeds.
Have well-defined incident response plans to handle security incidents quickly and effectively.
Prioritize the patching of critical software components like OpenSSL.

Case Study: The WannaCry Ransomware Attack

In 2017, the WannaCry ransomware attack exploited a critical zero-day vulnerability in Microsoft's Windows operating system. The attack spread rapidly, crippling computers and demanding ransom payments from victims.

The WannaCry attack highlighted the significance of:

Patching known vulnerabilities promptly, especially those affecting widely used operating systems.
Implementing network segmentation to limit the spread of malware.
Having effective incident response plans to contain the spread of an attack.
Staying informed about emerging cyber threats and vulnerabilities.

Case Study: The Equifax Data Breach

In 2017, Equifax, a major credit reporting agency, suffered a massive data breach that exposed the personal information of millions of consumers. The breach was attributed to a combination of factors, including a failure to patch a known vulnerability in the Apache Struts software framework, a popular web application framework.

The Equifax data breach highlighted the importance of:

Patching known vulnerabilities promptly, even those affecting third-party software.
Implementing robust security practices, including vulnerability management and data loss prevention.
Having well-defined incident response plans to address security incidents effectively.
Conducting regular security audits to identify and remediate vulnerabilities.

The journey to mitigate zero-day threats is an ongoing process that demands constant adaptation and vigilance. By staying informed about emerging threats, implementing robust security practices, and embracing innovative technologies, organizations can build a stronger defense against the ever-evolving landscape of cybersecurity threats.

The Foundation of a Secure Posture

The foundation of a secure posture starts with a deep understanding of the principles that underpin cybersecurity. It's not just about deploying fancy technology or hiring expensive experts; it's about creating a robust and layered defense that considers every aspect of your digital ecosystem.

Imagine a castle, surrounded by moats, fortified walls, and vigilant guards. The castle itself is your data, the moats represent your firewalls and network security measures, the walls are your intrusion detection systems, and the guards are your security personnel. Just as a castle can be breached if one of these defenses fails, so too can your data be compromised if your cybersecurity posture is weak in any area.

The first principle of a secure posture is **proactive security** . This means taking preventative measures to prevent breaches from happening in the first place. This involves implementing strong passwords and multi-factor authentication, keeping software and operating systems updated, and training employees on cybersecurity best practices. Imagine it like reinforcing the castle walls, ensuring they are strong enough to withstand any attack.

The second principle is **layered security** . This means implementing multiple security measures, each designed to stop different types of attacks. Like the castle's moat, walls, and guards, each layer provides an additional barrier to entry for attackers. Think of a firewall blocking unauthorized access to your network, an intrusion detection system alerting you to suspicious activity, and anti-malware software preventing malicious code from infiltrating your systems.

The third principle is **continuous monitoring** . This involves constantly monitoring your systems for signs of suspicious activity. This can be achieved through security information and event management (SIEM) tools, intrusion detection systems (IDS), and regular security audits. Imagine the castle's guards constantly patrolling the perimeter, watching for any signs of an approaching enemy.

The fourth principle is **incident response** . This involves having a plan in place for responding to security incidents, such as a data breach or malware infection. This plan should include steps for containing the damage, investigating the incident, and restoring your systems to their original state. Just like a well-trained army responding to an attack, a robust incident response plan can help minimize damage and ensure a quick recovery.

The fifth principle is **risk management** . This involves identifying, analyzing, and mitigating the risks posed to your organization's cybersecurity. It's about understanding the threats you face, assessing the potential impact of those threats, and implementing appropriate security measures to reduce the likelihood of a breach. Think of it like a castle's strategists, anticipating potential threats and strategizing to counter them.

The sixth principle is **compliance** . This involves meeting industry standards and regulations for data security. Depending on your industry and the type of data you handle, you may be subject to specific compliance requirements. This is like ensuring the castle meets the standards of the kingdom, demonstrating its strength and resilience.

Implementing these principles effectively requires a holistic approach, integrating them into every aspect of your organization.

Here's a real-world example:

Imagine a large financial institution, responsible for protecting sensitive customer data.

Proactive Security: They implemented a strong password policy, requiring all employees to use complex passwords and multi-factor authentication to access sensitive systems.

Layered Security: They deployed a robust firewall to block unauthorized access to their network, installed an intrusion detection system to alert them to suspicious activity, and implemented endpoint security software on all employee computers to prevent malware infections.

Continuous Monitoring: They used SIEM tools to analyze security logs and detect any unusual activity, and they conducted regular vulnerability scans to identify potential weaknesses in their systems.

Incident Response: They developed a comprehensive incident response plan, including detailed procedures for containing a breach, isolating affected systems, and restoring operations.

Risk Management: They conducted regular risk assessments to identify and prioritize the threats facing their organization, and they implemented controls to mitigate these risks.

Compliance: They adhered to industry regulations such as PCI DSS for handling payment card data, ensuring they met all requirements for protecting sensitive financial information.

By integrating these principles into their cybersecurity strategy, the financial institution created a robust defense against cyber threats, protecting their data and their customers.

Building a strong cyber defense is an ongoing process, requiring constant vigilance and adaptation to the ever-evolving threat landscape. The principles outlined here provide a foundation for building a secure posture, but it's crucial to stay updated on the latest threats and vulnerabilities, invest in ongoing training for employees, and continuously refine your security practices.

Think of it as a never-ending quest for security, constantly evolving and adapting to the changing dynamics of the digital world. Just like a castle constantly being reinforced and upgraded, your cybersecurity posture needs to be continually strengthened and modernized to stay ahead of the adversaries.

Layered Security Approaches

In the ever-evolving digital landscape, where cyber threats grow increasingly sophisticated, organizations are constantly striving to fortify their defenses. The concept of "defense-in-depth" emerges as a critical strategy for safeguarding networks and data from malicious actors. This layered approach aims to create multiple barriers, each with its own set of security controls, to hinder attackers from reaching their targets. By implementing a defense-in-depth strategy, organizations can significantly enhance their resilience against cyberattacks.

Imagine a castle surrounded by imposing walls, moats, and fortified towers. Each layer acts as a deterrent, making it progressively more challenging for invaders to penetrate the castle's defenses. Similarly, a defense-in-depth approach in cybersecurity involves creating a series of layers, each designed to prevent or mitigate specific types of attacks. This multi-faceted approach aims to frustrate attackers at every stage, making it significantly more difficult to achieve their objectives.

At the heart of defense-in-depth lies the principle of "failover," a mechanism that ensures the system continues functioning even if one layer is compromised. This redundancy is crucial in preventing a single point of failure from crippling the entire system. For instance, imagine a network with multiple firewalls, each inspecting traffic and blocking unauthorized access. If one firewall fails, the others can continue to protect the network, minimizing disruption.

The layered security approach involves several key components, each playing a vital role in the overall security posture:

1. Network Segmentation: Dividing the network into smaller, isolated segments helps limit the damage caused by a successful attack. Imagine a company's network divided into departments, each with its own firewall and access controls. If an attacker compromises one department, the damage remains confined to that segment, preventing the attacker from spreading laterally across the network.

2. Access Control: Restricting user access based on their roles and responsibilities is crucial in preventing unauthorized access to sensitive data. This can be achieved through user authentication, authorization, and least privilege principles. By granting users only the access they need to perform their jobs, organizations can significantly reduce the risk of data breaches.

3. Data Protection: Implementing data encryption, access control, and data loss prevention (DLP) mechanisms helps protect sensitive data from unauthorized access, use, or disclosure. This is particularly important for organizations handling sensitive information such as financial data, customer records, or intellectual property.

4. Endpoint Security: Protecting individual devices, such as laptops, workstations, and mobile phones, is essential in preventing attacks from spreading across the network. Endpoint security solutions, such as antivirus software, firewalls, and intrusion detection systems, play a crucial role in securing these devices.

5. Security Monitoring and Analysis: Continuously monitoring network traffic, user activities, and security logs is critical in detecting potential attacks and anomalies. Security Information and Event Management (SIEM) systems help collect, analyze, and correlate security data from various sources, providing a comprehensive view of the network's security posture.

6. Incident Response: Having a well-defined incident response plan is essential in minimizing the impact of a successful attack. This plan outlines the steps to be taken to contain the attack, remediate the damage, and restore normal operations. Effective communication and coordination among security teams are paramount in a successful incident response.

7. Security Awareness Training: Training users to recognize and avoid phishing attacks, malicious websites, and other social engineering techniques is crucial in preventing attackers from gaining unauthorized access to the network. Organizations should provide regular security awareness training to their employees, fostering a culture of security within the organization.

8. Patch Management: Regularly updating software with the latest security patches helps mitigate known vulnerabilities and prevents attackers from exploiting them. Organizations should establish a robust patch management process to ensure all systems are patched promptly and efficiently.

9. Backup and Recovery: Regularly backing up critical data and having a disaster recovery plan in place helps ensure the continuity of business operations in the event of a data loss incident. This enables organizations to restore data and systems quickly and efficiently, minimizing downtime and financial losses.

10. Security Audits and Assessments: Regularly conducting security audits and assessments helps identify potential vulnerabilities and weaknesses in the organization's security posture. These assessments provide a snapshot of the organization's security health, allowing for timely remediation of identified vulnerabilities.

Beyond these core components, defense-in-depth can incorporate various other measures depending on the organization's specific needs and risks. This could include:

Network Intrusion Detection Systems (NIDS): Detecting suspicious activity on the network and alerting security teams to potential threats.
Network Intrusion Prevention Systems (NIPS): Blocking suspicious traffic and preventing attacks from reaching their targets.
Web Application Firewalls (WAFs): Protecting web applications from attacks by filtering malicious traffic and blocking unauthorized access.
Security Information and Event Management (SIEM): Consolidating security data from various sources, providing a centralized platform for threat detection and analysis.
Security Orchestration, Automation, and Response (SOAR): Automating security tasks and workflows, improving efficiency and responsiveness.

The implementation of defense-in-depth requires a holistic approach, encompassing all aspects of the organization's technology infrastructure and operations. It's not just about deploying multiple security tools; it's about creating a comprehensive and integrated security framework that addresses the organization's unique risks and challenges.

To illustrate the effectiveness of defense-in-depth, let's consider a hypothetical scenario where a company has implemented a layered security approach:

Layer 1: Network Perimeter Security: The company has a firewall at its network perimeter, blocking unauthorized access from the internet. This layer prevents initial attempts by attackers to gain entry into the network.

Layer 2: Network Segmentation: The network is segmented into different zones, separating critical systems from less sensitive ones. If an attacker manages to bypass the perimeter firewall and gain access to one segment, they are prevented from accessing other areas of the network.

Layer 3: Endpoint Security: All company devices are equipped with antivirus software, firewalls, and intrusion detection systems. This layer prevents malware from infecting individual devices and spreading across the network.

Layer 4: Access Control: Users are only granted access to the systems and data they need to perform their jobs. This layer helps minimize the risk of unauthorized access to sensitive information.

Layer 5: Data Encryption: Sensitive data is encrypted both in transit and at rest, protecting it from unauthorized access even if the data is stolen.

Layer 6: Security Monitoring and Analysis: The company uses a SIEM system to monitor network traffic, user activities, and security logs, detecting suspicious behavior and identifying potential threats.

In this scenario, imagine an attacker attempting to infiltrate the company's network. They might initially attempt to bypass the perimeter firewall but fail due to the strong security controls in place. Even if they manage to gain access to one segment of the network, they are unable to spread laterally to other segments due to the network segmentation. The attacker might then attempt to exploit a vulnerability on one of the company's devices but fail because of the endpoint security measures in place. Finally, the attacker might try to access sensitive data but is prevented by the encryption and access controls implemented by the company.

This scenario demonstrates the effectiveness of defense-in-depth in creating a series of barriers, each making it progressively more challenging for an attacker to achieve their objectives. By combining multiple security layers, organizations can significantly enhance their resilience against cyberattacks, minimizing the impact of successful attacks and protecting their valuable assets.

While defense-in-depth is a powerful strategy, it's important to acknowledge that it's not a guaranteed solution. No security system is perfect, and attackers are constantly finding new ways to exploit vulnerabilities. It's crucial for organizations to stay vigilant, continuously updating their security practices and technologies to keep pace with the evolving threat landscape.

The implementation of defense-in-depth requires ongoing monitoring, assessment, and improvement. Organizations should regularly review their security posture, identify potential vulnerabilities, and implement necessary countermeasures. The security landscape is constantly changing, and staying ahead of emerging threats is essential in maintaining a robust security posture.

The story of Michael Anthony Trevino Jr., as detailed in "Shadows and Shields," highlights the importance of a layered security approach. Michael's journey as a red teamer taught him the value of understanding attackers' tactics and exploiting vulnerabilities. However, his mission ultimately became one of using his knowledge to fortify defenses, building strong cyber defenses for organizations. The insights he gained through his experience emphasize the need for a multi-faceted security strategy, incorporating a range of technologies and techniques to create a resilient defense against evolving threats.

By understanding the principles and techniques of defense-in-depth, organizations can take a significant step toward securing their networks and data in an increasingly perilous digital world. It's not about creating an impenetrable fortress, but about building a robust and adaptable defense that can withstand the onslaught of modern cyber threats. By implementing a layered security approach, organizations can significantly enhance their cybersecurity posture, ensuring the safety and integrity of their critical assets in the digital age.

Responding to Threats Effectively

In the realm of cybersecurity, a well-constructed defense is only as strong as its weakest link. While layered security measures provide a robust foundation, it's the ability to effectively respond to threats that truly sets a company apart. This is where the art of incident response comes into play, a critical element in safeguarding sensitive data and systems from malicious actors.

Imagine a scenario where a company's network is under attack. A skilled attacker has managed to bypass the initial line of defense, potentially exploiting a zero-day vulnerability, and is now deep within the system. This is when the incident response team springs into action.

Their first priority is **containment** . The goal is to prevent the attacker from spreading laterally within the network and causing further damage. This might involve isolating infected systems, blocking communication channels, and securing critical data repositories.

Think of this containment phase as a strategic retreat – a tactical maneuver to buy time and regain control of the situation.

Once containment is achieved, the team moves into **investigation** . They meticulously gather evidence of the attack, analyzing logs, network traffic, and system behavior to understand the attacker's tactics, objectives, and the extent of the damage. This investigative process is crucial for reconstructing the timeline of the intrusion, identifying vulnerabilities, and ultimately preventing similar attacks in the future.

The investigation is like a forensic analysis, piecing together the puzzle of the intrusion to understand the attacker's motives and techniques.

The final stage of incident response is **remediation** . This involves cleaning up the damage caused by the attack, restoring compromised systems, patching vulnerabilities, and implementing stronger security measures.

This remediation phase is akin to rebuilding a fortress, making it more robust and resilient against future threats.

Effective incident response goes beyond these basic steps. It requires a multifaceted approach, encompassing several key aspects:

1. A Comprehensive Incident Response Plan:

A well-defined incident response plan serves as the roadmap for handling security incidents. It outlines the roles and responsibilities of the incident response team, communication protocols, escalation procedures, and the steps to be taken in different scenarios. A robust plan provides a clear framework for action, reducing chaos and confusion during high-pressure situations.

Think of this plan as the company's playbook for handling cyberattacks, ensuring that everyone knows their role and how to respond effectively.

2. The Importance of Training and Drills:

Regular training and drills are essential for keeping the incident response team sharp and prepared. These exercises simulate real-world scenarios, allowing team members to practice their skills, refine their responses, and identify areas for improvement.

Just like fire drills, these exercises familiarize the team with the plan and help them react instinctively in an actual incident.

3. Effective Communication and Collaboration:

Clear and timely communication is paramount during a security incident. The incident response team must keep relevant stakeholders informed, including senior management, legal counsel, and law enforcement agencies. Collaboration with internal and external partners, such as cybersecurity vendors and security experts, is crucial for sharing information and leveraging expertise.

Imagine a symphony orchestra where each instrument plays a crucial role in creating a harmonious sound. In an incident response, effective communication ensures that each team member is on the same page, working in unison to achieve a common goal.

4. Automation and Orchestration:

In today's fast-paced digital landscape, automation plays a vital role in incident response. Automated tools can help with tasks such as threat detection, analysis, containment, and remediation, allowing the team to focus on strategic decisions.

Automation is like a high-powered tool that amplifies the team's capabilities, enabling them to act quickly and efficiently.

5. The Role of Threat Intelligence:

Threat intelligence is a crucial ingredient in effective incident response. By staying informed about the latest threats, attack vectors, and attacker tactics, the team can anticipate potential attacks, proactively strengthen defenses, and respond more effectively to incidents.

Think of threat intelligence as a spy network, providing critical insights into the adversary's tactics and movements.

Real-World Examples

To illustrate the importance of effective incident response, let's delve into some real-world examples:

a. The Target Data Breach (2013)

In 2013, Target, a major retail chain, suffered a massive data breach that compromised the personal information of millions of customers. The attackers exploited a vulnerability in Target's HVAC system to gain access to the network. While Target had a security team in place, the incident response was hampered by a lack of clear communication, delayed action, and inadequate automation.

This case highlights the critical need for robust incident response capabilities and the potential consequences of failing to respond effectively.

b. The Equifax Data Breach (2017)

Equifax, a major credit reporting agency, experienced a massive data breach in 2017, exposing the sensitive personal information of millions of individuals. The attackers exploited a known vulnerability in Equifax's software, which the company had failed to patch promptly. The incident response was further hindered by delays in notifying affected customers and a lack of transparency.

This case underscores the importance of prioritizing vulnerability management, prompt patching, and effective incident response communication.

c. The WannaCry Ransomware Attack (2017)

The WannaCry ransomware attack, which spread rapidly across the globe in 2017, exploited a vulnerability in Microsoft's Windows operating system. Many organizations were caught off guard, as they had failed to patch the vulnerability. While some companies responded effectively, others struggled to contain the spread of the ransomware. This case highlights the critical role of staying informed about emerging threats, patching vulnerabilities promptly, and having a well-defined incident response plan.

These real-world examples demonstrate the devastating impact of poorly managed security incidents and the importance of investing in robust incident response capabilities.

Moving Forward

In the ever-evolving landscape of cybersecurity, the need for effective incident response is only increasing. The rise of sophisticated attackers, emerging threats, and the interconnectedness of digital systems demand a proactive and well-prepared approach. By embracing the principles outlined above, companies can build strong incident response capabilities, mitigating risks, and safeguarding their digital assets.

Just as a skilled general prepares for battle, companies must equip themselves with the necessary tools, training, and strategies to effectively respond to cyber threats. This proactive approach is crucial for ensuring the resilience and security of businesses in the digital age.

The Role of Threat Intelligence

Threat intelligence is the lifeblood of any effective cybersecurity strategy. It's the process of gathering, analyzing, and disseminating information about potential cyber threats, allowing organizations to anticipate, prepare for, and neutralize attacks. This crucial practice involves understanding the motivations, tactics, and capabilities of adversaries, as well as identifying emerging vulnerabilities and trends within the constantly evolving digital landscape.

Imagine a chess game. A skilled chess player doesn't simply move their pieces randomly; they study their opponent's moves, anticipate their strategies, and plan accordingly. Similarly, in the world of cybersecurity, threat intelligence acts as the chess player's "intel," providing crucial insights into the strategies and tactics of cyber adversaries. This information allows organizations to proactively strengthen their defenses, identify potential attack vectors, and develop targeted countermeasures.

The process of gathering threat intelligence involves a multitude of sources. Open-source intelligence (OSINT), readily available information from public sources like news articles, social media posts, and forums, provides valuable insights into the activities of malicious actors. Specialized threat intelligence platforms and vendors offer curated reports and analysis based on their extensive research and monitoring of known threats.

However, it's crucial to go beyond the surface level. Deep-dive investigations, analyzing suspicious network traffic, malware samples, and even dark web forums can reveal the intricate details of an adversary's operations, including their technical capabilities, target preferences, and communication methods. This level of detail can be crucial in crafting a comprehensive and effective defense strategy.

The analysis of threat intelligence involves using a diverse range of tools and techniques. Data mining, statistical analysis, and machine learning algorithms are employed to identify patterns and anomalies within vast amounts of data. Analysts examine adversary tactics, techniques, and procedures (TTPs), mapping out the typical methods used in different types of attacks. This analysis helps to predict potential attack paths, understand the motivations behind attacks, and identify the specific tools and vulnerabilities often exploited by attackers.

The dissemination of threat intelligence is critical to ensure that relevant information reaches the right people within an organization. It's essential to provide tailored reports and summaries, specific to the organization's unique security needs and risk profile. These reports should clearly articulate the potential threats, recommended countermeasures, and the urgency of action required.

Effective threat intelligence is more than just gathering and disseminating information. It's about actively using this knowledge to inform strategic decisions, improve incident response capabilities, and develop a proactive approach to cybersecurity. This includes:

Proactive Vulnerability Management: Threat intelligence provides insight into commonly exploited vulnerabilities, enabling organizations to prioritize patching efforts and strengthen their defenses against known weaknesses. This proactive approach helps to minimize the impact of attacks and reduces the window of opportunity for adversaries.

Tailored Security Policies and Procedures: By understanding the specific threats targeting an organization, security policies and procedures can be customized to address these vulnerabilities. This ensures that resources are allocated effectively, and appropriate security measures are in place to mitigate the most significant risks.

Improved Incident Response: Threat intelligence helps to quickly identify and categorize the nature of an attack, guiding incident responders to deploy the most appropriate tools and techniques for containment and recovery. It also provides insights into the adversary's objectives and potential future actions, aiding in the development of mitigation strategies.

Michael, with his deep understanding of hacking tactics and techniques honed under the guidance of Kevin Mitnick, exemplifies the value of threat intelligence. He had a unique perspective on the motives, capabilities, and strategies of attackers. This knowledge was instrumental in his ability to anticipate and counter threats, ultimately making him a formidable defender in the digital realm.

Let's take a closer look at a few examples of how Michael's understanding of threat intelligence helped him build strong cyber defenses for his clients.

One of Michael's clients, a major financial institution, was facing a growing threat from sophisticated phishing attacks targeting their employees. Michael, drawing upon his knowledge of the tactics used by phishers, identified several vulnerabilities within the organization's email infrastructure and employee training programs. He recommended implementing stronger authentication protocols, enhancing phishing detection mechanisms, and conducting comprehensive employee awareness training on recognizing and avoiding phishing scams.

Another client, a global tech company, was struggling with zero-day vulnerabilities in their mobile applications. Michael, drawing upon his expertise in exploiting mobile operating systems, helped the company develop a multi-layered security strategy, including robust vulnerability scanning, rapid patch deployment, and rigorous code review practices. This proactive approach ensured that any emerging zero-day exploits targeting their mobile applications were identified and neutralized before they could cause significant harm.

However, threat intelligence is not a one-time endeavor. It requires continuous monitoring, adaptation, and refinement as the threat landscape evolves. The strategies that were effective today may not be sufficient tomorrow, as adversaries constantly develop new tactics and exploit emerging vulnerabilities. Therefore, organizations must continuously monitor threat intelligence feeds, update their security measures, and remain vigilant in protecting their digital assets.

The effectiveness of threat intelligence hinges on a fundamental principle: the ability to act on the information gathered. It's not enough to simply collect data; it's essential to analyze it, distill actionable insights, and implement appropriate countermeasures. This requires close collaboration between cybersecurity teams, threat intelligence analysts, and senior leadership, ensuring that everyone is aligned on the identified risks and the steps needed to mitigate them.

In conclusion, threat intelligence serves as a powerful tool in the fight against cyber threats. By understanding the motivations, capabilities, and tactics of adversaries, organizations can proactively strengthen their defenses, predict potential attacks, and respond swiftly and effectively to incidents. It is a crucial element of any comprehensive cybersecurity strategy, enabling organizations to stay ahead of the curve and navigate the ever-evolving digital landscape with greater confidence.

Continuous Improvement in Security

In the dynamic world of cybersecurity, the pursuit of a robust defense isn't a one-time endeavor. It's a continuous journey, an ever-evolving dance with the ever-present threat landscape. Just as adversaries refine their tactics, so too must defenders adapt and innovate to stay ahead of the curve. This continuous improvement is the cornerstone of building a truly formidable security posture.

Imagine a fortress, its walls seemingly impenetrable, but over time, erosion sets in. The elements weaken the structure, and vulnerabilities arise, creating inroads for attackers. The same principle applies to cybersecurity. Even the most intricate security measures can become outdated or compromised over time, leaving gaps that malicious actors can exploit. This is where the concept of continuous improvement takes center stage.

Think of it as a perpetual cycle of assessment, adaptation, and fortification. It involves regular vulnerability assessments, penetration testing, and security audits – a thorough examination of your defenses, searching for any cracks in the armor. These assessments aren't just about identifying weaknesses; they're about understanding the potential impact of those vulnerabilities and prioritizing remediation efforts.

Imagine a cybersecurity team conducting a vulnerability scan of a company's network. They uncover a critical flaw in a widely used software application. This vulnerability, if exploited, could allow an attacker to gain control of sensitive data or even cripple the company's operations. The team doesn't stop at simply identifying the flaw. They delve deeper, analyzing the potential attack vectors, the severity of the risk, and the likelihood of exploitation. Based on this analysis, they prioritize the remediation effort, ensuring that the most critical vulnerabilities are addressed first.

This cycle doesn't end with assessment. It's about taking action, patching vulnerabilities, implementing new security controls, and continuously refining your defenses. Imagine a company implementing multi-factor authentication across its systems. This security control adds an extra layer of protection, requiring users to provide multiple forms of authentication before granting access. This simple step, while seemingly minor, significantly strengthens their security posture, making it much harder for attackers to compromise accounts.

The key to continuous improvement is staying informed about the latest threats and vulnerabilities. Threat intelligence plays a crucial role in this process. By monitoring threat actors, their tactics, and the ever-evolving landscape of exploits, cybersecurity teams can proactively anticipate potential attacks. Imagine a team receiving intelligence on a new ransomware campaign targeting businesses in their industry. With this intelligence, they can bolster their defenses, implement specific security controls, and prepare for the possibility of an attack.

But it's not just about technology. Continuous improvement also involves fostering a culture of security awareness within the organization. Employees, often the weakest link in the security chain, play a vital role in defending against cyber threats. Regular security training, phishing simulations, and awareness campaigns are crucial in educating employees about potential risks and empowering them to make informed decisions.

Imagine a company running a phishing simulation, sending realistic phishing emails to employees. Some employees, lured by the deceptive emails, click on malicious links or provide sensitive information. This simulation, while seemingly a test, serves a crucial purpose. It exposes vulnerabilities in the company's security awareness, revealing how easily employees can be tricked by phishing attacks. This data then informs targeted training programs, focusing on specific vulnerabilities and empowering employees to recognize and report phishing attempts.

Continuous improvement isn't a one-size-fits-all approach. Each organization has its unique security challenges and vulnerabilities. The key is to tailor your continuous improvement strategy to your specific needs and risks. This involves understanding your organization's critical assets, evaluating your current security posture, and identifying areas for improvement. It also involves incorporating a risk-based approach, prioritizing remediation efforts based on the impact and likelihood of potential threats.

Imagine a financial institution, with its sensitive customer data being a prime target for attackers. Their continuous improvement strategy would focus heavily on protecting this data, implementing robust security controls for their systems, and conducting regular penetration testing to identify vulnerabilities. On the other hand, a small non-profit organization might have less sensitive data but could be vulnerable to phishing attacks. Their continuous improvement strategy would prioritize employee training and awareness campaigns, equipping their staff to recognize and report phishing attempts.

The world of cybersecurity is constantly evolving, with new threats emerging and old tactics being refined. Continuous improvement is the essential key to navigating this dynamic landscape. By embracing this philosophy, organizations can build a truly robust and resilient security posture, effectively defending against the ever-present cyber threats.

Defining Ethics in Cybersecurity

In the labyrinthine world of cybersecurity, where digital shadows dance and shields clash, ethics serve as the guiding light, illuminating the path for ethical hackers and cybersecurity professionals alike. This intricate dance between technical prowess and moral responsibility forms the bedrock of Michael's journey, shaping his every action as he navigates the perilous landscape of the digital realm.

Ethics in cybersecurity are not mere theoretical constructs but living principles that guide every decision, every line of code, and every vulnerability assessment. They are the invisible force that separates those who seek to exploit weaknesses for personal gain from those who leverage their skills to protect and defend.

Michael's journey is a testament to the power of ethical hacking. He honed his skills under the tutelage of Kevin Mitnick, a legendary figure in the world of cybersecurity who embraced the ethical hacker's creed. Mitnick, once a notorious hacker himself, realized the profound impact of using his knowledge for good. He understood that the same skills that could be used to wreak havoc could also be harnessed to strengthen security and protect individuals and organizations.

Michael embraced this philosophy wholeheartedly. He saw the immense potential in leveraging his technical abilities to safeguard the digital world. He believed that true mastery in cybersecurity lay not just in exploiting vulnerabilities but in understanding them, predicting them, and ultimately preventing them.

The ethical hacker's dilemma is a constant companion, a recurring question that challenges the very essence of their work. On one hand, they are tasked with uncovering vulnerabilities, often in intricate systems designed to be impenetrable. They are expected to think like an attacker, to anticipate their moves, and to exploit weaknesses before the real enemy can. But on the other hand, they are sworn to use their knowledge responsibly, to act as guardians of the digital realm, and to safeguard the interests of those they serve.

This delicate balance is not always easy to maintain. Ethical hackers are often forced to make difficult decisions, to weigh the potential consequences of their actions, and to navigate the murky waters of ethical gray areas. They must constantly grapple with the question: how far is too far?

Michael's code of conduct, forged in the crucible of real-world experience, embodies the essence of ethical hacking. He believes in transparency, in clear and consistent communication, and in the pursuit of knowledge for the greater good. His ethical guidelines are rooted in the principles of non-malicious intent, respect for privacy, and responsible disclosure.

He firmly believes that the power of knowledge should be used to protect, not to harm. Every vulnerability he uncovers, every exploit he develops, is a stepping stone towards a more secure digital future. He sees himself not as a hacker, but as a protector, a guardian of the digital realm, dedicated to building stronger defenses and safeguarding the very foundations of our digital world.

Real-world scenarios provide a stark reminder of the importance of ethical decision-making in cybersecurity. Imagine a scenario where Michael discovers a critical vulnerability in a healthcare system, a vulnerability that could expose sensitive patient data to malicious actors. He has the knowledge to exploit this weakness, to potentially gain access to sensitive information, but he also understands the devastating consequences that could follow.

The ethical hacker's dilemma is not just a theoretical concept; it's a lived experience, a constant struggle between temptation and responsibility. Michael's ethical compass guides him towards the path of integrity. He chooses to responsibly disclose the vulnerability to the organization, allowing them to patch the flaw before it can be exploited by nefarious actors.

This decision underscores the profound impact of ethical hacking. It highlights the importance of transparency, communication, and collaborative efforts in building a more secure digital environment. Michael's actions demonstrate the power of ethical principles in guiding cybersecurity professionals, shaping their decisions, and ultimately protecting the digital world from harm.

Promoting a culture of ethics is not just an individual endeavor; it's a collective responsibility. Ethical hackers play a crucial role in fostering a culture of respect, transparency, and collaboration within the cybersecurity community. They are the bridge between vulnerability and resilience, between potential threats and robust defenses.

Michael's unwavering commitment to ethical hacking serves as a beacon of hope in the ever-evolving digital landscape. His journey exemplifies the power of ethical principles in shaping a safer, more secure, and ultimately, more responsible digital world. His story inspires aspiring cybersecurity professionals to embrace the ethical hacker's creed, to use their knowledge for good, and to become guardians of the digital realm, ensuring that the future of cybersecurity is anchored in integrity and accountability.

The Ethical Hackers Dilemma

The path of an ethical hacker is not paved with smooth, predictable terrain. It is a labyrinth of moral complexities, ethical quandaries, and the constant struggle to walk the fine line between offense and defense. As Michael delved deeper into the world of cybersecurity, he discovered that wielding the power of hacking for good was not a simple task. It demanded unwavering self-awareness, a steadfast ethical compass, and an unyielding commitment to protecting the digital realm.

His journey began with the mentorship of Kevin Mitnick, a legendary figure in the world of hacking. Kevin, a former black hat hacker who spent time in prison for his exploits, turned his life around and became a respected cybersecurity expert. He taught Michael the nuances of hacking, the art of exploiting vulnerabilities, and the importance of responsible use of such knowledge.

The ethical hacker's dilemma stems from the very nature of their work. They delve into the dark underbelly of the digital world, seeking out vulnerabilities, and exploiting them – but only with the express purpose of improving security. This often involves pushing the boundaries of what is considered acceptable, tiptoeing along a delicate tightrope between exploiting a system and causing harm.

One of the most challenging aspects of ethical hacking is the constant negotiation with the gray areas of the law. Ethical hackers often work within the confines of contracts, operating with clear boundaries established by their clients. However, the line between what is legal and what is considered ethically permissible can be blurry. For instance, a hacker tasked with finding vulnerabilities in a company's network might discover a flaw that could be exploited by a malicious actor. The hacker is obligated to report this flaw to the company, but there is often a temptation to exploit it themselves, particularly if they believe the company won't act on the information.

Michael faced such a dilemma early in his career. He was working on a project for a financial institution, attempting to penetrate their network to assess their security posture. During his assessment, he discovered a critical vulnerability that could allow hackers to steal sensitive financial data. The bank had dismissed the vulnerability as a minor concern. However, Michael knew the potential consequences were enormous, potentially leading to a massive data breach and financial losses.

Torn between his contract and his conscience, Michael wrestled with his options. He could follow the contract and report the vulnerability, knowing it might not be addressed promptly. Or, he could act unilaterally and exploit the vulnerability to prove its severity and force the bank to take immediate action.

Michael, guided by his ethical compass and commitment to protecting data, chose the latter. He crafted a sophisticated exploit that would simulate a real-world attack, highlighting the vulnerability's potential impact. He presented his findings to the bank's security team, accompanied by a compelling demonstration of the exploit. His actions forced the bank to acknowledge the seriousness of the vulnerability and implement immediate measures to mitigate the risk.

This experience deeply impacted Michael, solidifying his resolve to always prioritize ethical conduct and responsible use of his hacking skills. He realized that ethical hacking wasn't just about finding vulnerabilities but also about ensuring they were addressed effectively, ultimately protecting individuals and organizations from harm.

The ethical hacker's dilemma extends beyond legal complexities. It also involves navigating the complexities of human interaction and the potential for unintended consequences. Michael discovered that ethical hacking often required him to make difficult judgments, balancing the need for security against the potential impact on individuals and organizations.

In another instance, Michael was tasked with testing the security of a social media platform. His goal was to identify and report any vulnerabilities that could expose user data. However, during his assessment, he stumbled upon a flaw that could potentially allow him to access the private messages of users. This presented a moral dilemma: Should he exploit this vulnerability to prove its severity, even if it meant potentially violating the privacy of innocent users?

Michael decided to prioritize the privacy of users. He chose to report the vulnerability to the platform's security team without exploiting it, emphasizing the importance of protecting user data. He understood that while exposing the vulnerability was crucial for security, it could also lead to potential harm if misused.

Through his ethical journey, Michael learned that ethical hacking wasn't just about technical expertise. It was about responsible use of knowledge, navigating moral complexities, and making decisions that prioritized the well-being of individuals and the collective good.

The ethical hacker's dilemma is a constant companion on their journey. It is the invisible force that guides their actions, shaping their decisions, and reminding them that wielding the power of hacking comes with an immense responsibility. It is a testament to their commitment to using their knowledge for good, safeguarding the digital world, and building a more secure future for all.

Michaels Code of Conduct

Michael's journey through the labyrinthine world of cybersecurity was not just a quest for technical mastery but also a constant dance with ethical considerations. The knowledge he gleaned from Kevin Mitnick, a master of exploiting vulnerabilities, was a double-edged sword. It empowered him to identify weaknesses in systems but also instilled a profound understanding of the potential damage that could be unleashed.

Michael recognized that his skills could be used for both good and ill. This realization became a cornerstone of his professional life. He resolved to channel his talents towards protecting individuals and organizations from the very threats he could create. This commitment formed the basis of his personal ethical code, a guiding light that informed every decision he made as a cybersecurity expert.

Michael's code of conduct was not a rigid set of rules but a living document that evolved alongside his experience. It was based on three fundamental principles: **responsibility, integrity, and transparency** .

Responsibility lay at the heart of his code. He understood that the information he possessed, the exploits he crafted, and the insights he gained had immense power. He felt a deep sense of responsibility to use his knowledge to safeguard individuals and organizations from harm. He saw himself not just as a cybersecurity professional but as a guardian of the digital realm, tasked with protecting the vulnerable from the shadows that lurked within.

Integrity was paramount. Michael believed that ethical hacking, while a potent tool, should never be used for personal gain or malicious intent. He adhered to the highest standards of conduct, refusing to compromise his principles, even when faced with temptations or pressure. He viewed ethical hacking as a means to expose vulnerabilities, not exploit them. He felt a strong moral obligation to use his skills for the greater good, upholding the sanctity of information and the integrity of the digital landscape.

Transparency was the cornerstone of his approach. He believed in open communication and collaboration, sharing his findings responsibly with the wider cybersecurity community. This principle guided his interactions with clients and colleagues, ensuring that everyone understood the risks involved and the actions necessary to mitigate them. He advocated for a transparent ecosystem where vulnerabilities were exposed and addressed openly, fostering a collective effort to improve cybersecurity.

Michael's code of conduct was not merely an abstract set of ideals; it was a practical framework that guided his actions in every facet of his work. When presented with a new challenge, he would ask himself:

"Does this action align with my responsibility to protect individuals and organizations?"
"Am I compromising my integrity in any way?"
"Am I being transparent in my approach?"

If the answer to any of these questions was "no," he would re-evaluate his course of action. This rigorous self-assessment ensured that his skills were always wielded ethically, aligning with his commitment to responsible cybersecurity.

He often found himself in complex ethical situations, navigating the gray areas where the lines between ethical and unethical actions blurred. But Michael's code of conduct provided him with a clear compass, guiding him through these challenges and helping him make informed decisions.

One such instance occurred during his involvement in a penetration testing exercise for a major financial institution. He discovered a critical vulnerability in the bank's online platform, capable of granting unauthorized access to sensitive customer data.

The ethical dilemma arose when he realized the vulnerability was a zero-day exploit, meaning that the bank was completely unaware of it. He could have reported the flaw immediately, but this would have disrupted the bank's operations and potentially caused financial losses. On the other hand, keeping it secret and exploiting it could have been a lucrative opportunity.

Michael wrestled with this dilemma for days. He knew that exploiting the vulnerability would be a breach of his ethical code, but he also understood the financial implications of exposing it prematurely. Ultimately, he decided to report the vulnerability directly to the bank's security team, providing them with a detailed analysis and a proposed solution.

His decision was based on the principle of responsibility. He believed that it was his duty to inform the bank of the potential threat, even if it meant causing temporary disruption. He recognized that his actions could potentially cost the bank money, but he also understood that inaction would have cost them far more in the long run.

The bank was initially apprehensive about the discovery but ultimately appreciated Michael's honesty and professionalism. They implemented the recommended security measures, preventing a potentially catastrophic data breach.

This case study highlights the complexity of ethical decision-making in the realm of cybersecurity. It demonstrates how Michael's personal code of conduct served as a guide in navigating these complex situations, ensuring that he acted in a responsible, ethical, and transparent manner.

Michael's ethical journey was a testament to his commitment to responsible cybersecurity. He understood that true security was not just about building impenetrable defenses but also about cultivating a culture of ethics and integrity within the cybersecurity community. He believed that every individual had a role to play in safeguarding the digital realm, and he sought to inspire others to embrace the same principles that guided his work.

He became a mentor to aspiring cybersecurity professionals, sharing his knowledge and emphasizing the importance of ethical conduct. He advocated for the adoption of ethical frameworks within organizations and encouraged open dialogue about the challenges of ethical hacking.

Michael's ethical journey was not always easy. It required constant vigilance, self-reflection, and a willingness to challenge the status quo. But he remained steadfast in his commitment, believing that true cybersecurity could only be achieved when ethics were at the forefront.

His story is a powerful reminder that cybersecurity is not just a technical field but a moral one. It underscores the importance of ethical decision-making in an increasingly complex digital landscape. Michael's code of conduct serves as a blueprint for responsible cybersecurity, urging professionals to wield their knowledge and skills ethically and responsibly, protecting the digital world for the benefit of all.

Case Studies in Ethical Hacking

The world of cybersecurity is a complex and ever-evolving landscape, demanding not only technical proficiency but also a strong ethical compass. It's where the lines between right and wrong can blur, and where decisions made in the heat of the moment can have far-reaching consequences. As a seasoned ethical hacker, Michael Anthony Trevino Jr. navigated this world with a clear sense of purpose, driven by the desire to safeguard the digital realm. His journey was not just about acquiring technical mastery but also about embodying the core principles of ethical hacking.

One of Michael's defining moments came during a penetration test for a major financial institution. The client had entrusted Michael with the task of identifying vulnerabilities in their systems, and he had successfully unearthed a critical flaw in their authentication process. With his exploit, Michael could potentially gain unauthorized access to sensitive financial data, a scenario that could have had devastating consequences for the institution and its clients. However, Michael's unwavering commitment to ethical hacking prevented him from exploiting the vulnerability. Instead, he carefully documented his findings, presented them to the client's security team, and provided detailed recommendations for remediation.

The ethical choice Michael made in this situation exemplifies the fundamental principle of responsible hacking. It is a powerful reminder that the knowledge and skills possessed by ethical hackers are not to be abused but rather to be used for the betterment of society. This case study reveals the inner workings of Michael's ethical framework, where the pursuit of vulnerability discovery is balanced by a commitment to protecting individuals and institutions from harm.

In another instance, Michael was tasked with assessing the security of a global healthcare organization. During his investigation, he discovered a critical vulnerability in the organization's patient management system. This vulnerability could potentially have exposed the personal health information of thousands of patients to unauthorized access. Michael's ethical dilemma was compounded by the fact that the healthcare organization was in the midst of a pandemic, and any disruption to their systems could have had severe consequences for patients and healthcare providers alike.

Michael knew that he had a responsibility to disclose the vulnerability immediately to prevent a potential breach. However, he also understood the need to minimize disruption to the organization's critical operations. He carefully crafted his report, detailing the vulnerability and providing clear and actionable recommendations for its remediation. He also collaborated with the organization's security team to ensure a smooth and timely patch deployment, minimizing the impact on patient care.

This scenario showcases the importance of effective communication and collaboration in ethical hacking. Michael's commitment to transparency and responsible disclosure ensured that the vulnerability was addressed swiftly and efficiently, mitigating the risk of a potential data breach and protecting sensitive patient information. The ethical hacker's role extends beyond just identifying vulnerabilities; it also involves working in collaboration with the target organization to ensure their security posture is strengthened and their systems are better protected.

A particularly challenging ethical case involved Michael's engagement with a leading social media platform. During his penetration test, he discovered a critical flaw in the platform's user authentication system, allowing him to access the accounts of millions of users. This vulnerability, if exploited, could have allowed malicious actors to steal personal information, spread misinformation, and disrupt the platform's operations on a massive scale.

The ethical ramifications of such a vulnerability were immense. Michael was faced with a decision that could have far-reaching consequences for millions of users. While the temptation to exploit the vulnerability for personal gain might have been tempting, Michael's commitment to ethical hacking guided his actions. Instead of taking advantage of the flaw, he reported it to the platform's security team, providing detailed insights and recommendations for remediation. This act of responsible disclosure prevented a potential disaster, safeguarding the privacy and security of millions of users.

This case study highlights the critical role that ethical hackers play in safeguarding the digital world. They are not just technical experts; they are guardians of information security, committed to upholding ethical standards and protecting users from harm. This story underscores the importance of responsible vulnerability disclosure, emphasizing that ethical hackers are not merely seeking to exploit flaws but rather to identify and mitigate them, ensuring the security and integrity of the systems they evaluate.

Michael Anthony Trevino Jr.'s career as an ethical hacker was marked by his unwavering commitment to upholding the highest ethical standards. He understood that his skills and knowledge were a powerful tool that could be used for good or for evil. Through his actions, he demonstrated the importance of ethical hacking, not just as a set of technical skills but as a guiding principle that shapes every decision made by a cybersecurity professional. He believed that every action, no matter how small, had the potential to impact the digital world, and he made a conscious effort to ensure that his actions were guided by ethical considerations.

Michael's journey as an ethical hacker was not without its challenges and ethical dilemmas. He encountered scenarios where the lines between right and wrong blurred, where the temptation to exploit vulnerabilities for personal gain was strong, and where the potential consequences of his actions could have far-reaching implications. However, he consistently chose the ethical path, driven by a deep commitment to protecting individuals, institutions, and the digital world as a whole.

Michael's commitment to ethics was not merely an abstract principle but a guiding force that shaped his actions and decisions. He understood that ethical hacking was not about exploiting vulnerabilities for personal gain but rather about safeguarding the digital realm from those who would seek to exploit it. His work as an ethical hacker was a testament to his unwavering belief in the power of ethical hacking to create a safer and more secure digital world.

Michael's experiences highlight the critical role of ethical decision-making in cybersecurity. As the digital landscape continues to evolve and cyber threats become more sophisticated, the need for ethical hackers with a strong moral compass is paramount. These individuals are the gatekeepers of the digital world, ensuring that the power of technology is used for good and not for harm. Their commitment to ethical principles is not just a matter of personal choice but a critical factor in shaping the future of cybersecurity.

Michael's legacy extends beyond his technical expertise; it is a testament to the importance of ethical hacking as a force for good in the digital world. His story serves as an inspiration to aspiring cybersecurity professionals, reminding them that ethical principles are not just an afterthought but a fundamental cornerstone of their profession. In a world where the lines between right and wrong can blur, Michael's journey is a powerful reminder that ethical hacking is not just about technical skills but about making the right choices for the greater good.

Promoting a Culture of Ethics

Michael's journey wasn't just about mastering the tools of the trade. It was about understanding the profound responsibility that came with wielding such power. He had seen firsthand the potential for destruction that lurked within the digital shadows, and he was determined to use his skills for good. He knew that the world of cybersecurity wouldn't be safe until everyone embraced a culture of ethical hacking, where the lines between right and wrong were crystal clear. This wasn't simply about following a set of rules; it was about embodying a mindset that prioritized integrity and responsibility.

From the very beginning, Michael had instilled within himself a strong ethical compass. He understood that his actions had the power to impact countless individuals and organizations. Every exploit, every vulnerability, every line of code, carried a weight that he couldn't ignore. He had witnessed the destructive potential of unethical hacking firsthand, and he knew that the pursuit of personal gain or notoriety could have catastrophic consequences.

His dedication to ethical hacking wasn't a mere theoretical concept. It was a guiding principle that shaped every aspect of his work. He sought to use his skills for the betterment of society, believing that cybersecurity should be a force for good, not an instrument of chaos. His commitment to ethical practices wasn't a burden; it was a source of strength and purpose. It fueled his passion, driving him to excel in his craft, knowing that every success was a victory for the forces of security.

Michael's dedication extended beyond his own actions. He believed in cultivating a culture of ethical hacking within the entire cybersecurity community. He saw the need for open dialogue, where ethical considerations were at the forefront of every discussion. This wasn't about imposing his own views; it was about sparking meaningful conversations that would raise awareness and encourage responsible behavior.

He understood that the boundaries of ethical hacking were not always clear-cut. He had faced his own dilemmas, where the allure of uncovering hidden vulnerabilities clashed with his ethical principles. In these moments, he had relied on his core values, his intuition, and the wisdom of his mentor, Kevin Mitnick. He had learned that ethical hacking wasn't just about avoiding illegal activities; it was about navigating the complexities of the digital world with empathy, integrity, and a deep sense of responsibility.

Michael's vision for a more ethical cybersecurity landscape involved fostering a community where everyone, from seasoned professionals to aspiring students, felt empowered to act with integrity. He believed in the power of education, mentorship, and shared experiences to shape a culture of ethical conduct. His commitment to this vision wasn't a solitary pursuit; it was a collaborative endeavor, one that required the participation of everyone involved in the cybersecurity ecosystem.

He understood that ethical hacking wasn't just about individual actions; it was about collective responsibility. He sought to create a shared understanding of the ethical principles that guided the cybersecurity community, ensuring that every member felt accountable for their actions. This wasn't about creating a rigid set of rules; it was about fostering a culture where ethics permeated every aspect of the profession.

Michael knew that promoting a culture of ethics wasn't a one-time effort; it was an ongoing journey. He recognized that the challenges faced by cybersecurity professionals would continue to evolve, demanding new ethical considerations and approaches. He believed in the power of continuous learning and adaptation, ensuring that ethical principles remained relevant and responsive to the ever-changing digital landscape.

He saw the need for ongoing dialogue, where ethical considerations were woven into every aspect of cybersecurity discussions. This wasn't about policing boundaries; it was about fostering a sense of shared responsibility, where everyone felt empowered to speak up and challenge practices that fell short of ethical standards.

Michael's approach to promoting ethical hacking wasn't about moralizing or imposing his own views; it was about fostering open and inclusive conversations. He encouraged a culture of transparency and accountability, where ethical principles were discussed openly and honestly. He recognized that ethical dilemmas were often complex and nuanced, requiring thoughtful consideration and a willingness to engage in difficult discussions.

He understood that ethical hacking wasn't just about adhering to a set of rules; it was about embracing a mindset that prioritized responsible and ethical conduct. He saw the importance of developing ethical frameworks and guidelines that could provide clear direction for cybersecurity professionals navigating the complexities of their field. He also recognized the value of professional organizations and communities, where ethical discussions could be fostered and best practices could be shared.

Michael's vision for a more ethical cybersecurity landscape wasn't about achieving perfection; it was about continuous improvement. He believed in the power of collaborative efforts to address the challenges faced by the cybersecurity community. He recognized that everyone, from students to seasoned professionals, had a role to play in shaping a more ethical future for the digital world.

Michael's journey as a cybersecurity expert wasn't just about mastering technical skills; it was about embracing a profound sense of responsibility. He understood that the power to shape the digital landscape came with an obligation to use it for good. His commitment to ethical hacking extended beyond his own actions; he was a champion for a culture where integrity and responsibility were woven into the fabric of the cybersecurity community. He knew that building a safer digital world wasn't just about technological prowess; it was about ethical leadership, a vision that would guide the next generation of cybersecurity professionals.

Mentorship and Knowledge Transfer

The journey from a novice to a seasoned cybersecurity expert is often paved with challenges, but the guidance of experienced mentors can illuminate the path and accelerate growth. Mentorship is not just a transfer of technical skills; it's about fostering a deep understanding of the cybersecurity landscape, instilling ethical values, and nurturing a passion for defending the digital world.

Michael's journey with Kevin Mitnick exemplifies the transformative power of mentorship. Kevin, a legendary figure in the world of hacking, recognized Michael's raw talent and unwavering dedication. He became Michael's guide, sharing his vast knowledge, practical experience, and invaluable insights. Through their close bond, Michael absorbed not only technical expertise but also the ethical compass that would shape his career.

Mentorship goes beyond one-on-one interactions. It can take various forms, from structured programs to informal peer learning. Organizations and educational institutions are increasingly recognizing the value of mentorship in nurturing future cybersecurity talent.

Structured Mentorship Programs

Formal mentorship programs provide a framework for structured learning and development. These programs often involve pairing aspiring cybersecurity professionals with seasoned experts. The mentor acts as a guide, providing support, guidance, and constructive feedback.

Benefits of Structured Mentorship Programs:

Personalized Guidance: Mentors tailor their advice to the mentee's specific needs, goals, and areas of interest.

Skill Development: Mentors offer valuable insights and practical advice on developing essential cybersecurity skills, such as ethical hacking, vulnerability assessment, incident response, and security analysis.

Career Advancement: Mentors can provide insights into career paths, networking opportunities, and professional development strategies.

Networking Opportunities: Structured programs often facilitate networking events, connecting mentees with a broader community of cybersecurity professionals.

Informal Mentorship and Peer Learning

While structured programs offer valuable frameworks, informal mentorship and peer learning play a vital role in shaping cybersecurity expertise.

Benefits of Informal Mentorship and Peer Learning:

Sharing Practical Knowledge: Informal mentorship allows for the exchange of real-world experience, insights, and lessons learned.

Collaborative Problem-Solving: Peer learning fosters a collaborative environment where individuals can work together to solve complex cybersecurity challenges.

Networking and Community Building: Informal mentorship and peer learning contribute to the formation of strong professional networks and support communities.

The Role of Industry Organizations and Educational Institutions

Industry organizations and educational institutions play a critical role in fostering mentorship and knowledge transfer.

Industry Organizations:
Professional Development Programs: Industry organizations offer professional development programs, including mentorship initiatives, to enhance cybersecurity skills and knowledge.
Conferences and Events: Cybersecurity conferences and events provide platforms for networking, knowledge sharing, and mentoring opportunities.
Certification Programs: Industry certifications serve as benchmarks of cybersecurity expertise, motivating individuals to seek mentorship and guidance.

Educational Institutions:
Cybersecurity Curriculum: Educational institutions are increasingly integrating cybersecurity into their curriculum, offering specialized programs and courses.
Faculty Mentorship: Experienced faculty members in cybersecurity programs often act as mentors, providing guidance and support to students.
Industry Partnerships: Educational institutions partner with cybersecurity companies and organizations to offer internships, research opportunities, and mentoring programs.

Fostering Innovation and Collaboration

Mentorship is not only about transferring existing knowledge; it's also about fostering innovation and collaboration in the cybersecurity field. Mentors can encourage mentees to explore new ideas, develop creative solutions, and embrace emerging technologies.

Innovation in Cybersecurity:
Emerging Technologies: Mentors can guide mentees to understand the implications of emerging technologies, such as artificial intelligence (AI) and machine learning (ML), for cybersecurity.

Research and Development: Mentorship can encourage research and development of innovative cybersecurity tools, techniques, and strategies.
Ethical Hacking Competitions: Mentorship can support participation in ethical hacking competitions, where individuals can hone their skills and explore cutting-edge techniques.

Collaborative Networks:
Open-Source Communities: Mentors can encourage mentees to contribute to open-source cybersecurity projects, fostering collaboration and knowledge sharing.
Industry Partnerships: Mentorship can facilitate collaboration between cybersecurity professionals, researchers, and industry experts.
Cybersecurity Forums and Communities: Mentors can encourage mentees to engage in cybersecurity forums and online communities, fostering discussion, knowledge sharing, and collaboration.

Inspiring the Next Generation of Cyber Guardians

Mentorship plays a vital role in inspiring the next generation of cybersecurity professionals. Mentors serve as role models, showcasing the impact and importance of a career in cybersecurity.

Attracting Young Talent: Mentors can share their passion for cybersecurity, inspiring young individuals to pursue careers in this field.
Mentoring Programs for Students: Mentorship programs targeting high school and college students can introduce them to cybersecurity concepts and career opportunities.
Promoting Diversity and Inclusion: Mentorship can play a role in promoting diversity and inclusion in the cybersecurity

workforce, ensuring that all talented individuals have the opportunity to thrive.

Beyond Technical Expertise: Nurturing Ethical Values

Mentorship is not just about transferring technical skills; it's also about shaping ethical values and fostering a sense of responsibility.

Ethical Hacking Principles: Mentors guide mentees to understand the ethical principles that govern ethical hacking, emphasizing the importance of respect for privacy, confidentiality, and the law.
Responsible Disclosure: Mentors teach the importance of responsible disclosure, where vulnerabilities are reported to the appropriate parties in a timely and ethical manner.
Ethical Decision-Making: Mentors help mentees develop their ethical decision-making skills, enabling them to navigate complex moral dilemmas in the cybersecurity landscape.

Conclusion

Mentorship is a cornerstone of cybersecurity excellence. It is a powerful force that empowers individuals, fosters innovation, and shapes the future of the cybersecurity field. By investing in mentorship programs and fostering a culture of knowledge transfer, we can equip the next generation of cyber warriors with the skills, ethical values, and passion needed to protect the digital world. The journey from novice to cybersecurity expert is a collaborative endeavor, and the guidance of experienced mentors makes all the difference.

Training the Next Generation

The journey of a cybersecurity professional isn't just about mastering technical skills; it's about nurturing the next generation of digital guardians. The world of cybersecurity is constantly evolving, and to stay ahead of the curve, we need to empower future professionals with the knowledge, tools, and inspiration to become the next line of defense. This is where the crucial role of mentorship and knowledge transfer comes into play.

Imagine a young, aspiring cybersecurity professional, eager to learn and make a difference. This is where experienced professionals like Michael step in, sharing their expertise and guiding these individuals on their own paths. Mentorship isn't just about imparting technical knowledge; it's about fostering a love for the field, nurturing critical thinking skills, and instilling a sense of responsibility. It's about creating a supportive network where aspiring cyber warriors can learn from each other, share experiences, and grow together.

But beyond mentorship, we need to provide aspiring professionals with structured educational pathways and resources. There's a wealth of information available online, from online courses and certifications to specialized bootcamps and university programs. This abundance of resources caters to different learning styles and preferences, allowing individuals to tailor their education to their specific interests and career goals.

Let's take a closer look at some of the most effective training pathways for aspiring cybersecurity professionals:

1. Formal Education: Universities and colleges offer comprehensive cybersecurity degree programs, equipping students with a foundational understanding of computer science, networking, cryptography, and ethical hacking. These programs delve into advanced concepts like penetration testing, incident response, and risk management, preparing students for a wide range of cybersecurity roles.

2. Professional Certifications: Industry-recognized certifications, such as Certified Ethical Hacker (CEH), Certified Information Systems Security Professional (CISSP), and CompTIA Security+, validate an individual's expertise and demonstrate their commitment to professional development. These certifications are often highly sought after by employers, enhancing job prospects and career advancement opportunities.

3. Online Learning Platforms: Platforms like Coursera, Udemy, and Udacity offer a vast selection of online cybersecurity courses, catering to diverse learning needs. These courses provide flexibility and accessibility, allowing individuals to learn at their own pace and convenience. Many platforms offer specialized courses focusing on specific areas of cybersecurity, such as web security, mobile security, or cloud security.

4. Cyber Security Boot Camps: These intensive programs offer hands-on training and practical experience in a condensed timeframe. Bootcamps are designed to bridge the gap between theory and practice, equipping participants with real-world skills and immediate job readiness.

5. Community Engagement: Joining professional organizations like the International Information Systems Security Certification Consortium (ISC)² or the SANS Institute provides access to valuable resources, networking opportunities, and continuing education programs. These communities foster collaboration and knowledge sharing, helping aspiring professionals stay updated with the latest cybersecurity trends and best practices.

The journey of a cybersecurity professional is a lifelong pursuit of knowledge and skills. It requires a continuous effort to adapt to evolving threats and stay ahead of the curve. To inspire and empower the next generation of cyber guardians, we need to create a supportive ecosystem that nurtures their passion, guides their learning, and provides them with the tools and resources they need to succeed.

Let's delve deeper into the importance of fostering innovation in cybersecurity. As cyber threats become more sophisticated, we need to encourage innovative thinking and creative solutions to stay ahead of the game. This means promoting research, developing new technologies, and encouraging collaboration across different fields.

1. Encouraging Research: Universities and research institutions play a pivotal role in driving innovation in cybersecurity. Funding research projects focused on emerging threats, vulnerability analysis, and developing novel security solutions is crucial for advancing the field.

2. Developing New Technologies: Investing in research and development (R&D) of cutting-edge cybersecurity technologies, such as AI-powered threat detection systems, blockchain-based security solutions, and quantum-resistant cryptography, is essential for staying ahead of adversaries.

3. Fostering Cross-Disciplinary Collaboration: Cybersecurity is no longer a siloed field. Collaboration across disciplines, such as computer science, engineering, psychology, and social sciences, is essential for developing comprehensive solutions to complex cybersecurity challenges.

4. Promoting Ethical Hacking: Ethical hacking, also known as penetration testing, plays a vital role in identifying vulnerabilities and strengthening cybersecurity defenses. Encouraging ethical hacking competitions and initiatives can help nurture the skills and creativity of future cyber professionals.

5. Supporting Open Source Projects: Open source communities contribute significantly to cybersecurity innovation by sharing code, tools, and best practices. Supporting open source projects and encouraging participation in these communities fosters collaboration and accelerates the development of new solutions.

Building collaborative networks is another crucial aspect of empowering future cyber guardians. These networks provide a platform for aspiring professionals to connect with experienced mentors, industry experts, and peers. They offer opportunities for knowledge sharing, collaboration, and mentorship, fostering a sense of community and shared purpose.

1. Professional Networking Events: Conferences, workshops, and meetups provide platforms for cybersecurity professionals to connect, exchange ideas, and build relationships. Attending these events offers opportunities for learning, networking, and career advancement.

2. Online Communities and Forums: Online forums, social media groups, and online communities dedicated to cybersecurity provide valuable resources, support, and networking opportunities for aspiring professionals. They allow for the exchange of knowledge, best practices, and industry insights.

3. Mentorship Programs: Formal mentorship programs connect aspiring cybersecurity professionals with experienced mentors who provide guidance, support, and career advice. These programs create valuable relationships that foster professional growth and development.

4. University and College Cybersecurity Clubs: Cybersecurity clubs provide students with a platform to connect with peers, participate in hands-on projects, and engage in industry-relevant activities. These clubs offer opportunities for networking, skill development, and career exploration.

5. Hackathons and Capture the Flag (CTF) Competitions: Hackathons and CTF competitions offer a platform for aspiring professionals to test their skills, collaborate with peers, and develop innovative solutions to cybersecurity challenges. These events foster creativity, teamwork, and problem-solving skills.

Inspiring a new wave of defenders is essential for ensuring the digital security of our future. It's about captivating young minds with the excitement of the cybersecurity field, showcasing the impact they can make, and demonstrating the rewarding career paths available.

1. Engaging Educational Programs: Incorporating interactive cybersecurity modules into school curriculums can spark interest and introduce young students to the concepts and challenges of cybersecurity.

2. STEM Outreach Programs: STEM outreach programs, such as workshops, hackathons, and coding camps, can provide hands-on experiences and inspire students to pursue careers in STEM fields, including cybersecurity.

3. Cybersecurity Awareness Campaigns: Raising awareness about cybersecurity issues through public service announcements, media campaigns, and community events can highlight the importance of digital security and inspire young people to get involved.

4. Role Models and Mentorship: Highlighting the achievements and experiences of successful cybersecurity professionals can inspire young people to pursue careers in this field. Mentorship programs can provide guidance and support to aspiring cybersecurity professionals.

Empowering future cyber guardians is a collective responsibility. It requires a collaborative effort from educators, industry leaders, mentors, and the broader cybersecurity community. By nurturing the next generation of digital defenders, we can ensure a future where the digital world is a safer and more secure place for everyone.

Fostering Innovation in Security

The world of cybersecurity is constantly evolving, with new threats emerging faster than we can imagine. To stay ahead of the curve, we need to encourage innovative thinking, fostering an environment where creative solutions can flourish. This is where the next generation of cyber guardians steps in. We need to empower them with the tools, knowledge, and mindset to tackle the challenges that lie ahead.

One key strategy is to foster a culture of mentorship and knowledge transfer. Experienced cybersecurity professionals have invaluable experience and insights that can guide the next generation. By actively engaging in mentorship programs, sharing best practices, and nurturing talent, we can create a pipeline of highly skilled cyber defenders.

Educational pathways are crucial in shaping future cybersecurity experts. Universities, colleges, and online learning platforms should offer comprehensive programs that cover the latest technologies and techniques. These programs should go beyond technical skills, emphasizing critical thinking, problem-solving, and ethical considerations.

Innovation in cybersecurity is not just about developing new technologies; it's about pushing the boundaries of our thinking. We need to encourage a culture of experimentation and exploration, where unconventional approaches are embraced. This means encouraging researchers to delve into emerging threats, develop innovative security tools, and explore novel ways to defend against attacks.

Hackathons, competitions, and research grants can be powerful tools for fostering innovation. These initiatives provide a platform for aspiring cyber warriors to showcase their skills, collaborate with peers, and develop groundbreaking solutions. By providing opportunities for young professionals to test their ideas, we can uncover hidden talents and accelerate the pace of innovation.

Building collaborative networks is essential for fostering a vibrant cybersecurity ecosystem. By connecting cybersecurity professionals, researchers, industry leaders, and government agencies, we can create a shared knowledge base and facilitate cross-pollination of ideas. This collaboration can lead to the development of shared solutions and the rapid deployment of new security measures.

Inspiring young professionals to pursue careers in cybersecurity is crucial. We need to highlight the importance of this field and the impact it has on our lives. By showcasing successful cybersecurity professionals, highlighting the challenges and rewards of the profession, and fostering a culture of respect and recognition, we can attract a new wave of talent to the cybersecurity arena.

This new generation of cyber guardians must be equipped to face the evolving landscape of cyber threats. They need to be adaptable, creative, and ethical in their approach to cybersecurity. We must empower them with the tools, knowledge, and support they need to be the guardians of our digital future.

The Role of Education and Training

The foundation of a strong cybersecurity workforce lies in education and training. Traditional cybersecurity programs have been instrumental in equipping professionals with the skills and knowledge they need. However, the ever-changing landscape of cybersecurity demands a more dynamic and adaptable approach to education.

Educational institutions need to embrace the latest technologies and incorporate them into their curriculum. Courses on machine learning, artificial intelligence, blockchain, and cloud security should be integrated into cybersecurity programs to equip students with the skills necessary to navigate this evolving digital environment.

Beyond technical skills, it's crucial to cultivate critical thinking and problem-solving abilities in aspiring cybersecurity professionals. They need to be able to analyze complex security threats, identify vulnerabilities, and develop innovative solutions. Simulation-based training, real-world case studies, and ethical hacking exercises can help students hone these essential skills.

Embracing New Technologies

The rise of artificial intelligence (AI) and machine learning (ML) has ushered in a new era of cybersecurity. These technologies can automate repetitive tasks, analyze massive datasets to detect anomalies, and predict potential threats.

AI and ML are already being deployed in a wide range of cybersecurity applications, including intrusion detection and prevention systems, threat intelligence platforms, and malware analysis tools. As these technologies continue to evolve, they will play an even more critical role in enhancing our cyber defenses.

However, it's essential to acknowledge the ethical considerations surrounding the use of AI in cybersecurity.

We need to ensure that these technologies are deployed responsibly, transparently, and without compromising human rights.

The Importance of Collaboration

The global nature of cybersecurity threats necessitates a collaborative approach to defense. Sharing information, best practices, and threat intelligence is essential for building a robust cybersecurity ecosystem.

Government agencies, private sector companies, research institutions, and cybersecurity professionals must work together to combat cyber threats. This collaboration can take various forms, including joint investigations, threat information sharing initiatives, and collaborative research projects.

By fostering collaboration and knowledge sharing, we can create a stronger and more resilient cybersecurity community.

The Human Factor

While technology plays a crucial role in cybersecurity, the human factor remains a critical element. Employees are often the weakest link in any organization's security posture. They can be tricked into clicking on malicious links, falling for social engineering attacks, or inadvertently exposing sensitive information.

Therefore, cybersecurity awareness training is essential. Employees must be educated about common cyber threats, best practices for online security, and the importance of reporting suspicious activities. This training should be ongoing, ensuring that employees stay informed about the latest threats and vulnerabilities.

The Future of Cybersecurity

The cybersecurity landscape is in a constant state of flux, with new threats emerging and technologies evolving at a rapid pace. As we look towards the future, it's essential to anticipate the challenges and opportunities that lie ahead.

The increasing integration of technology in our lives, the rise of the Internet of Things (IoT), and the growing reliance on cloud computing create new vulnerabilities that require proactive cybersecurity measures. We must embrace these technologies while ensuring their secure implementation.

The development of quantum computing presents both potential benefits and risks for cybersecurity. While it could enhance our ability to break encryption algorithms, it also presents new opportunities for cybercriminals to conduct attacks. We need to prepare for the advent of quantum computing and develop new encryption methods that are resistant to quantum attacks.

A Call to Action

The future of cybersecurity depends on our collective efforts to empower the next generation of cyber guardians. By fostering innovation, promoting collaboration, and prioritizing education, we can create a more secure digital world for all.

We must encourage young people to pursue careers in cybersecurity, inspiring them to become the defenders of our digital future. Together, we can build a cybersecurity ecosystem that is resilient, adaptable, and capable of safeguarding our online world.

Building Collaborative Networks

In the world of cybersecurity, where the lines between offense and defense blur, collaboration becomes an essential tool for survival. Just like a lone warrior standing against an army, individual cybersecurity professionals can only achieve so much. The power lies in joining forces, sharing knowledge, and building a collective defense against the ever-evolving tide of cyber threats. This is where professional networks and communities play a crucial role.

Imagine a bustling marketplace where cybersecurity experts gather, not to trade goods, but to exchange ideas, strategies, and experiences. These networks act as hubs of knowledge, allowing individuals to connect, learn from one another, and collaborate on solutions. The exchange of information, both technical and strategic, fosters innovation, strengthens defenses, and empowers future generations of cyber guardians.

One of the most significant benefits of these networks is the ability to learn from the collective experience of others. Cybersecurity is a dynamic field, constantly evolving as attackers refine their tactics and technology advances at an unprecedented pace. No single individual can possess the knowledge and expertise required to stay ahead of the curve. By engaging in collaborative networks, cybersecurity professionals gain access to a vast pool of knowledge, diverse perspectives, and real-world insights.

Imagine a cybersecurity expert facing a complex technical challenge, struggling to identify the root cause of a vulnerability. Through a professional network, they can tap into the expertise of their peers, seeking guidance, insights, and even potential solutions. Perhaps a seasoned veteran has encountered a similar issue in the past, sharing their knowledge and helping the novice navigate the intricacies of the problem. This collaborative approach not only accelerates problem-solving but also fosters a sense of community and support within the cybersecurity field.

Beyond technical knowledge, professional networks facilitate the exchange of best practices and industry standards. These shared guidelines help to standardize security approaches, ensuring a consistent level of protection across different organizations. Imagine a scenario where a company discovers a new type of malware, leveraging a previously unknown vulnerability. By sharing this information within a professional network, other organizations can be alerted to the threat, allowing them to implement preventative measures before falling victim. This collaborative approach to threat intelligence significantly enhances the overall security posture of the entire cybersecurity community.

Furthermore, these networks provide a platform for mentorship and knowledge transfer. Senior cybersecurity professionals, veterans with years of experience in the field, can guide and mentor aspiring newcomers, sharing their wisdom and guiding them through the intricacies of cybersecurity. This invaluable mentorship helps to foster a new generation of skilled and ethical cybersecurity professionals, ensuring the continuation of knowledge and expertise within the field.

Imagine a young cybersecurity student eager to enter the workforce, but lacking the practical experience required to land a job. By joining a professional network, they can connect with seasoned mentors who provide guidance, practical advice, and potential career opportunities. These mentorship relationships not only help newcomers gain valuable experience but also foster a sense of camaraderie and support within the cybersecurity community.

The power of professional networks extends beyond knowledge sharing and mentorship. These platforms also facilitate the development of new tools, methodologies, and technologies. By bringing together individuals with diverse skills and perspectives, these networks create a fertile ground for innovation. Imagine a group of cybersecurity researchers, each with their own expertise, collaborating on a new security solution. This collective effort, driven by a shared passion for cybersecurity, could lead to groundbreaking advancements that improve the digital security landscape for everyone.

The concept of building a collaborative network extends beyond the traditional confines of professional organizations. Open-source communities, online forums, and cybersecurity conferences all serve as platforms for knowledge sharing, collaboration, and innovation. These digital spaces provide a global forum where cybersecurity professionals can connect, learn from one another, and contribute to a collective effort towards a more secure digital future.

One example of the power of open-source communities is the development of security tools. Open-source projects, driven by a collaborative effort of volunteers, have produced some of the most powerful and effective security tools available today. These tools, freely available to the public, empower both cybersecurity professionals and individuals to protect themselves against cyber threats. This collaborative approach to security tool development fosters innovation, democratizes security, and strengthens the collective defense against cyberattacks.

The importance of building collaborative networks in cybersecurity cannot be overstated. These platforms act as catalysts for knowledge sharing, innovation, and mentorship, empowering future generations of cyber guardians to tackle the ever-evolving landscape of cyber threats. By fostering a sense of community, collaboration, and shared purpose, these networks build a stronger defense against the forces of darkness lurking in the digital realm.

As Michael Anthony Trevino Jr. learned throughout his career, the power of collaboration cannot be underestimated. He witnessed firsthand the importance of connecting with others, sharing insights, and learning from the collective wisdom of the cybersecurity community. This spirit of collaboration, interwoven with a dedication to ethical practices, played a pivotal role in his journey to become a respected cyber security expert.

The story of Michael's journey through the cybersecurity landscape serves as a testament to the power of collaboration. By embracing the interconnectedness of the field, leveraging the knowledge and expertise of others, and contributing to the collective effort, Michael and others like him can make a significant difference in the fight to secure the digital realm.

In the end, the power of collaborative networks lies in their ability to unite individuals with a shared goal – to protect the digital world. As we navigate the complexities of the cyber landscape, the strength of our collective defense will be determined by the strength of our collaborative efforts.

Inspiring a New Wave of Defenders

The world of cybersecurity is constantly evolving, and with each passing day, new challenges and threats emerge. The need for skilled and dedicated cybersecurity professionals is greater than ever before, and inspiring the next generation of defenders is crucial in shaping a safer digital future.

Michael's journey, as documented in this book, embodies the spirit of dedication and commitment that inspires countless young minds. His mentorship and guidance have proven invaluable to aspiring cybersecurity professionals, fostering a new wave of talent driven by passion and ethical principles.

The Power of Mentorship

Mentorship plays an indispensable role in nurturing the growth of future cyber guardians. It provides a bridge between experienced professionals and aspiring individuals, offering invaluable guidance, practical insights, and a sense of camaraderie. Michael, through his mentorship of aspiring hackers and security professionals, has exemplified the profound impact that mentorship can have on shaping careers.

His approach to mentorship is characterized by a blend of technical expertise and personal encouragement. He readily shares his knowledge, experience, and even his own vulnerabilities, creating an environment of trust and open communication. By making himself accessible and providing real-world examples, Michael helps his mentees understand the complexities of cybersecurity and the challenges they might face.

The most effective mentorship often transcends the mere transmission of knowledge. It fosters a sense of purpose and a commitment to ethical practice. Michael's mentorship instills in his mentees not only the technical skills required but also the ethical framework essential for navigating the moral dilemmas inherent in cybersecurity.

The Call to Action: Pursuing a Career in Cybersecurity

Motivating young professionals to embark on a career in cybersecurity requires a multi-pronged approach that addresses both the intellectual curiosity and the sense of purpose that drives individuals.

The Appeal of the Challenge

Cybersecurity is an intellectually stimulating field that attracts those who thrive on problem-solving, critical thinking, and the thrill of uncovering hidden vulnerabilities. The constant evolution of cyber threats presents a dynamic landscape, where knowledge and skills must continually adapt and grow. This inherent challenge appeals to individuals who seek intellectually stimulating careers.

The Significance of Impact

Beyond the intellectual appeal, cybersecurity offers a profound sense of purpose. The field provides an opportunity to make a real difference in the world by protecting individuals, organizations, and critical infrastructure from cyberattacks. The impact of cybersecurity professionals on the safety and security of our digital lives is tangible and profound.

The Power of Role Models

Exemplary figures like Michael, who combine technical brilliance with ethical commitment, serve as powerful role models for aspiring cybersecurity professionals. Their stories inspire and demonstrate the transformative power of cybersecurity, encouraging others to embrace the challenges and rewards of the field.

The Future of Cybersecurity Education

The need for skilled cybersecurity professionals is expanding at an exponential rate, necessitating a comprehensive and adaptive approach to education. Universities and educational institutions are stepping up to meet this demand, offering a wide array of cybersecurity programs designed to cultivate the next generation of defenders.

Academic Pathways to Cybersecurity

The traditional route to a cybersecurity career often involves pursuing a degree in computer science, information technology, or cybersecurity itself. These programs provide a solid foundation in computer programming, networking, security principles, and ethical hacking techniques.

Hands-On Learning and Certifications

In addition to traditional academic programs, a growing number of educational institutions offer hands-on learning opportunities, boot camps, and certifications that provide practical skills and real-world experience. These programs often incorporate capture the flag (CTF) competitions and real-world hacking exercises, allowing students to develop their skills in a safe and controlled environment.

The Importance of Continuous Learning

The field of cybersecurity is constantly evolving, with new threats and vulnerabilities emerging regularly. Continuous learning is essential for staying ahead of the curve. This can involve attending industry conferences, pursuing professional certifications, reading industry publications, and participating in online communities where knowledge is shared and best practices are discussed.

Cultivating a Culture of Collaboration

Collaboration is the lifeblood of cybersecurity. By fostering strong networks and communities, cybersecurity professionals can collectively combat threats and share insights, leading to a more secure digital landscape.

Professional Organizations and Communities

The cybersecurity industry boasts a robust network of professional organizations and communities that serve as platforms for knowledge sharing, collaboration, and networking. These organizations often host conferences, workshops, and webinars, bringing together experts from various sectors of the industry.

The Power of Open Source

Open-source communities play a significant role in advancing cybersecurity knowledge and fostering collaboration. Open-source tools, frameworks, and resources are often developed and shared by a global network of cybersecurity enthusiasts, contributing to the collective advancement of the field.

Sharing Best Practices

The sharing of best practices, lessons learned, and security vulnerabilities is crucial to enhancing the overall security posture of the industry. This collaborative approach ensures that knowledge is disseminated widely, enabling organizations to learn from past mistakes and implement more effective security measures.

Inspiring a New Wave of Defenders

The future of cybersecurity relies on a steady influx of talented and passionate professionals. Inspiring young minds to embrace cybersecurity as a career path requires a multifaceted approach that addresses their curiosity, values, and aspirations.

Emphasizing the Societal Impact

The importance of cybersecurity transcends the realm of technology. It has a direct impact on society, protecting individuals, businesses, and critical infrastructure from cyberattacks. Highlighting this societal impact can be a powerful motivator for aspiring cybersecurity professionals.

Providing Mentorship and Guidance

Mentorship plays a crucial role in nurturing the next generation of cybersecurity professionals. Experienced professionals can guide aspiring individuals, share their knowledge, and provide practical insights into the field. Mentorship programs and initiatives can help foster a sense of community and support.

Creating Educational Opportunities

Expanding access to quality cybersecurity education is essential in developing a robust talent pool. This can involve offering scholarships, creating hands-on learning opportunities, and providing resources for students interested in pursuing cybersecurity careers.

Promoting Ethical Hacking

Ethical hacking, also known as penetration testing, provides a valuable pathway for aspiring cybersecurity professionals to gain practical experience and develop their skills in a controlled environment. Ethical hacking competitions and programs can foster innovation and a spirit of competition within the industry.

Embracing Diversity and Inclusion

A diverse and inclusive cybersecurity workforce is essential for tackling complex threats. Creating an environment where individuals from all backgrounds feel welcomed and supported can foster creativity, innovation, and a more robust cybersecurity ecosystem.

The challenge of safeguarding our digital world requires a dedicated and passionate workforce. Inspiring a new wave of defenders requires a multi-pronged approach that fosters curiosity, promotes ethical practice, and highlights the societal impact of cybersecurity. By embracing mentorship, fostering collaboration, and creating opportunities for aspiring professionals, we can ensure a future where robust cybersecurity protects our digital lives and empowers us to thrive in a rapidly evolving digital landscape.

Anticipating Future Threats

The future of cybersecurity is a landscape riddled with uncertainty, a constantly shifting terrain where new threats emerge with alarming regularity. To navigate this evolving world, we must not only understand the threats of today but also anticipate the challenges of tomorrow. The ever-increasing sophistication of cyberattacks, fueled by advancements in artificial intelligence (AI), quantum computing, and the internet of things (IoT), presents a daunting prospect.

One of the most significant future threats lies in the realm of AI-powered attacks. Malicious actors are increasingly leveraging AI to automate and enhance their operations. Imagine a future where AI-driven phishing campaigns tailor their messages with uncanny accuracy, exploiting individual vulnerabilities and social engineering techniques to bypass even the most robust security measures. These attacks could become more personalized and targeted, making them harder to detect and defend against.

Moreover, the convergence of AI and quantum computing poses a significant threat. Quantum computers have the potential to break modern encryption algorithms, rendering current security protocols obsolete. This breakthrough could have devastating consequences, potentially unlocking sensitive data stored across the internet, from financial records to national security secrets. The implications are far-reaching, impacting every aspect of our digital lives.

The rise of the IoT is another crucial factor shaping the future of cybersecurity. As billions of devices connect to the internet, each one becomes a potential entry point for attackers. This interconnected ecosystem creates vast attack surfaces, making it difficult to secure every device effectively. Imagine a scenario where a malicious actor compromises a smart home system, gaining control of security cameras, locks, and even appliances, potentially putting lives at risk.

The ever-evolving nature of ransomware attacks is also a concern. The evolution of ransomware from simple extortion schemes to sophisticated attacks involving data exfiltration and denial-of-service (DoS) presents a complex challenge. These attacks are becoming more targeted, with attackers focusing on critical infrastructure and essential services, potentially disrupting entire industries and economies.

The rise of social engineering attacks further complicates the cybersecurity landscape. As social media and online platforms become increasingly intertwined with our daily lives, attackers are exploiting these channels to gain access to sensitive information. Imagine a scenario where a highly sophisticated deepfake video tricks a company executive into releasing confidential data or transferring funds. These attacks leverage human vulnerabilities and exploit our trust in the digital world.

The implications of these future threats are far-reaching. They could impact critical infrastructure, compromise national security, disrupt financial markets, and even endanger lives. The potential for widespread chaos and disruption is a stark reality, underscoring the need for proactive and comprehensive cybersecurity strategies.

To address these emerging threats, the cybersecurity community must adapt and evolve. The focus must shift from reactive defense to proactive threat hunting and prevention. This requires embracing new technologies and strategies, such as:

AI-driven security solutions: Implementing AI-powered systems to analyze vast amounts of data, detect anomalies, and identify potential threats in real time.

Quantum-resistant cryptography: Developing new encryption algorithms that are resistant to attacks from quantum computers, ensuring the security of sensitive data in the future.

Secure IoT development practices: Implementing robust security measures during the design and development of IoT devices, minimizing vulnerabilities and securing the entire interconnected ecosystem.

Enhanced threat intelligence sharing: Fostering collaboration among cybersecurity professionals and organizations to share threat information and best practices, improving overall security posture.

Cybersecurity awareness training: Educating users about cybersecurity threats and best practices, empowering them to make informed decisions and protect themselves against cyberattacks.

The future of cybersecurity is not just about technology; it's about human resilience and adaptability. We must cultivate a culture of security consciousness, where individuals and organizations are actively engaged in safeguarding the digital world. This requires fostering a sense of collective responsibility, recognizing that cybersecurity is not just an IT concern but a shared endeavor.

As we navigate the future of cybersecurity, we must embrace innovation, collaboration, and a deep understanding of the ever-evolving threats. Only by doing so can we create a secure and resilient digital future for all.

The Evolution of Cyber Defense

The landscape of cybersecurity is a dynamic and ever-evolving arena, constantly adapting to the relentless innovation of cybercriminals. This constant evolution is driven by factors such as the increasing complexity of technology, the proliferation of interconnected devices, and the growing sophistication of cyberattacks. As we navigate this ever-changing landscape, understanding the evolution of cyber defense is crucial to building resilient and secure digital infrastructures.

One of the most significant advancements in cybersecurity has been the shift from traditional, perimeter-based security models to a more proactive and layered approach. Historically, organizations relied heavily on firewalls, intrusion detection systems (IDS), and antivirus software to protect their networks from external threats. However, as cyberattacks became increasingly sophisticated, targeting vulnerabilities within applications and exploiting human error, this perimeter-centric approach proved insufficient. The evolution of cyber defense has seen a move towards a more holistic approach, encompassing a broader range of security controls and methodologies.

A cornerstone of this evolution is the adoption of threat intelligence, which plays a pivotal role in anticipating and mitigating cyber threats. Threat intelligence goes beyond reactive measures, focusing on proactively understanding the motives, tactics, and capabilities of adversaries. By analyzing data from various sources, such as open-source intelligence, malware analysis, and incident response reports, organizations can gain valuable insights into emerging threats and adapt their security strategies accordingly.

The integration of artificial intelligence (AI) and machine learning (ML) has also revolutionized cyber defense. These technologies have the potential to automate repetitive tasks, enhance threat detection capabilities, and improve decision-making in real-time. AI-powered security solutions can analyze vast amounts of data to identify anomalies and suspicious activity, enabling faster detection and response to cyberattacks. However, the use of AI in cybersecurity also raises concerns regarding potential biases and vulnerabilities, requiring careful consideration of ethical implications and robust safeguards.

Another crucial aspect of the evolving cyber defense landscape is the increasing emphasis on human factors. While technology plays a vital role in security, the human element remains a critical vulnerability. Phishing attacks, social engineering, and insider threats highlight the importance of cybersecurity awareness and training. Organizations need to invest in educating employees about best practices, fostering a culture of security, and promoting a proactive approach to reporting potential threats.

The rise of cloud computing has also significantly impacted cybersecurity. Cloud-based services have become integral to many businesses, offering scalability, flexibility, and cost-effectiveness. However, this shift presents new challenges for security professionals, as data and applications are distributed across different environments and infrastructure. Organizations need to adopt cloud-native security solutions, ensuring secure access, data encryption, and compliance with relevant regulations.

The evolving nature of cyber threats necessitates a continuous cycle of improvement and adaptation. Organizations must regularly assess their security posture, identify weaknesses, and implement appropriate countermeasures. Penetration testing, vulnerability scanning, and red teaming exercises are valuable tools for identifying vulnerabilities and simulating real-world attacks, enabling organizations to strengthen their defenses.

As we move forward into the future of cybersecurity, the evolution of cyber defense will continue to be driven by the constant arms race between attackers and defenders. Emerging technologies like blockchain, quantum computing, and the Internet of Things (IoT) will introduce new security challenges and opportunities. The ability to adapt, innovate, and collaborate will be paramount to navigating this complex and ever-changing landscape.

In conclusion, the evolution of cyber defense is a continuous journey, driven by the relentless innovation of cybercriminals and the constant need to adapt and improve security strategies. From the shift to layered security models and the adoption of threat intelligence to the integration of AI and ML and the focus on human factors, the cybersecurity landscape has undergone significant transformations. As we navigate the future of cybersecurity, understanding this evolution is essential to building resilient and secure digital infrastructures, protecting ourselves and our digital assets from the ever-evolving threat landscape.

Cybersecurity Policy and Legislation

The landscape of cybersecurity is constantly evolving, driven by the relentless innovation of technology and the ever-changing tactics of cybercriminals. As we look ahead, the role of policy and legislation becomes increasingly critical in shaping the future of cybersecurity. These frameworks act as the guiding principles that define acceptable behavior, establish accountability, and foster a safer digital environment.

One of the most significant impacts of policy and legislation is the standardization of security practices. Regulations like the General Data Protection Regulation (GDPR) and the California Consumer Privacy Act (CCPA) have imposed stringent requirements on organizations regarding data protection and privacy. These regulations compel companies to implement robust security measures, conduct regular audits, and establish clear data breach notification protocols. This standardization fosters a culture of responsibility, pushing organizations to elevate their security posture beyond mere compliance to a proactive stance of safeguarding sensitive information.

Beyond data privacy, cybersecurity policy extends to critical infrastructure protection, national security, and cybercrime prevention. Governments around the world are enacting laws and regulations to address the growing threat of cyberattacks targeting essential services, such as energy grids, financial institutions, and transportation systems. This emphasis on critical infrastructure security reinforces the need for collaborative efforts between the public and private sectors, with governments providing guidance and enforcement mechanisms while industry leaders contribute their expertise and resources to build resilient systems.

Furthermore, the legal landscape surrounding cybersecurity is constantly evolving. As new threats emerge, legislation adapts to address them effectively. For instance, the increasing prevalence of ransomware attacks has led to the development of laws focusing on the identification, apprehension, and prosecution of ransomware perpetrators. These legal frameworks aim to deter malicious actors, create deterrents for cybercrime, and provide avenues for victims to seek compensation or recovery.

In addition to traditional legal frameworks, the rise of international cooperation is also shaping cybersecurity policy. Countries are recognizing that cyber threats transcend borders and require coordinated efforts to combat them effectively. This has led to the creation of international agreements and organizations dedicated to sharing information, developing best practices, and fostering collaborative investigations. The Global Cybersecurity Forum and the United Nations' Cybersecurity Strategy are examples of such initiatives, promoting a unified front against cyber threats.

However, the complex nature of cybersecurity presents challenges for policy and legislation. One key issue is the constant race between lawmaking and technological advancements. By the time new laws are enacted, the digital landscape may have shifted significantly, rendering the regulations outdated or ineffective. This necessitates a dynamic approach to policymaking, with regular updates and revisions to stay abreast of evolving technologies and cyber threats.

Another challenge lies in balancing security with privacy and freedom. While stringent security measures can help protect individuals and organizations, they also raise concerns about the potential for government overreach or infringement on personal liberties. Striking a balance between security and privacy requires careful consideration of societal values, individual rights, and the potential for misuse of power.

In addition to the legal and policy aspects, the role of education and awareness plays a crucial role in shaping the future of cybersecurity. As technology becomes increasingly sophisticated, it's vital to empower individuals with the knowledge and skills to protect themselves online. This includes fostering digital literacy, promoting responsible online behavior, and educating individuals about common threats and prevention techniques.

The future of cybersecurity will be shaped by a complex interplay of technology, policy, and societal factors. While advancements in AI and automation offer opportunities to enhance defenses, they also create new vulnerabilities that require careful consideration. As we navigate this evolving landscape, it is crucial to prioritize a holistic approach that encompasses robust security measures, effective legislation, strong international collaboration, and a well-informed and empowered citizenry.

Ultimately, the success of cybersecurity hinges on building a culture of responsibility and collaboration, where individuals, organizations, and governments work together to ensure a safe and secure digital future for all.

The Role of AI and Automation

The future of cybersecurity is inextricably linked to the relentless march of technology, and at the forefront of this revolution lies the transformative power of artificial intelligence (AI) and automation. As the digital landscape evolves at an unprecedented pace, AI and automation are emerging as potent tools to enhance cybersecurity defenses and outmaneuver the ever-evolving tactics of cybercriminals. This section will delve into the profound impact of AI and automation on the cybersecurity landscape, exploring their strengths, limitations, and the potential they hold to shape a more secure digital future.

Imagine a scenario where an AI-powered security system can identify and neutralize sophisticated cyberattacks in real time, before they even have a chance to inflict damage. This is no longer a futuristic fantasy; it is becoming a tangible reality with the advent of AI-driven security solutions. AI algorithms can analyze massive datasets of security events, patterns, and indicators of compromise (IoCs), identifying subtle anomalies and suspicious activities that might otherwise escape human detection. They can learn from past attacks, adapt to new threats, and anticipate future vulnerabilities, providing a proactive layer of defense against a constantly evolving threat landscape.

One of the key areas where AI is making a significant impact is in the realm of threat detection and response. AI-powered security information and event management (SIEM) systems are revolutionizing the way organizations analyze and respond to cyberattacks. These systems can process vast volumes of security logs, identify potential threats, and trigger automated responses, such as blocking malicious traffic or isolating infected systems. AI can also be used to detect and prevent insider threats, identifying unusual user behavior patterns that might indicate malicious intent.

Beyond threat detection, AI is also being deployed to enhance other aspects of cybersecurity, such as vulnerability assessment and risk management. AI algorithms can scan vast codebases for vulnerabilities, identifying potential security flaws that might be missed by traditional security tools. They can also analyze network traffic patterns, predict potential attacks, and prioritize security resources based on the level of risk.

The integration of AI and automation is also transforming the way security teams operate. By automating routine tasks, such as vulnerability patching, malware analysis, and security incident reporting, AI frees up security professionals to focus on more strategic and complex tasks, such as threat intelligence analysis and incident response planning. This not only improves efficiency but also enables security teams to be more proactive in their approach to cybersecurity.

However, while AI offers significant advantages in cybersecurity, it is important to recognize that it is not a silver bullet. AI systems are only as good as the data they are trained on, and they can be susceptible to adversarial attacks aimed at manipulating or poisoning their training data. Moreover, the ethical implications of using AI in cybersecurity must be carefully considered. There is a need to ensure that AI-powered security solutions are used responsibly and do not infringe on privacy or civil liberties.

Despite these challenges, the potential of AI and automation in cybersecurity is undeniable. By leveraging the power of these technologies, organizations can build more resilient and proactive security defenses that are capable of keeping pace with the ever-evolving threat landscape. As the world becomes increasingly interconnected and reliant on digital technologies, it is essential that we embrace the transformative power of AI and automation to secure our digital future.

The Role of AI in Cybersecurity:

1. Threat Detection and Response:

Enhanced Threat Intelligence: AI algorithms can analyze vast amounts of data from various sources, such as security logs, threat feeds, and open-source intelligence, to identify patterns and anomalies that indicate potential threats. By correlating data from different sources, AI can uncover complex attack chains and reveal hidden connections that might escape human detection. This enhanced threat intelligence enables organizations to be more proactive in anticipating and mitigating threats.

Real-Time Threat Detection: AI-powered intrusion detection systems (IDS) and intrusion prevention systems (IPS) can analyze network traffic in real time, identifying suspicious activity and triggering automated responses. These systems use machine learning algorithms to learn normal network behavior and detect deviations that could indicate malicious activity. By identifying threats in real time, AI systems can prevent attacks from reaching their targets or minimize the damage they cause.

Automated Incident Response: AI-powered security orchestration and automation platforms (SOAR) streamline incident response processes by automating routine tasks. They can collect and analyze data from various sources, identify the affected systems, and trigger automated actions, such as isolating infected devices or blocking malicious IP addresses. This automation allows security teams to respond to incidents faster and more efficiently, minimizing downtime and reducing the impact of attacks.

Zero-Trust Security: AI can be used to implement zero-trust security models, which assume that no user or device can be trusted by default. AI algorithms can continuously monitor user activity and system behavior, identifying anomalies that could indicate malicious activity. This approach helps to prevent unauthorized access and data breaches, even from internal users.

2. Vulnerability Management and Patching:

Automated Vulnerability Assessment: AI-powered vulnerability scanners can analyze vast codebases, identifying potential security weaknesses that might be missed by traditional security tools. These scanners use machine learning algorithms to learn from known vulnerabilities and identify similar patterns in new code. This enables organizations to identify and address vulnerabilities faster, reducing the risk of exploitation.

Prioritization of Vulnerabilities: AI algorithms can analyze vulnerability data and prioritize them based on their severity, likelihood of exploitation, and impact on the organization. This enables security teams to focus on the most critical vulnerabilities first, improving the efficiency of their patching efforts.

Automated Patching: AI can automate the process of patching vulnerabilities by identifying the appropriate patches, scheduling updates, and deploying them across the organization. This reduces the risk of human error and ensures that systems are patched in a timely manner, minimizing the risk of exploitation.

3. User Behavior Analytics (UBA):

Detecting Insider Threats: AI algorithms can analyze user activity data, identifying unusual patterns that could indicate insider threats. These patterns can include accessing sensitive data without authorization, working outside of normal hours, or making changes to system configurations without proper approval. By identifying these anomalies, AI can help organizations to mitigate the risk of insider threats.

Fraud Detection: AI-powered fraud detection systems can analyze transactions and user behavior patterns to identify potential fraudulent activity. These systems can identify unusual spending patterns, identify forged documents, and detect suspicious account activity. This helps organizations to prevent financial losses and protect their customers from fraud.

4. Security Automation:

Streamlining Security Operations: AI can automate routine security tasks, such as vulnerability scanning, malware analysis, and security incident reporting. This frees up security professionals to focus on more strategic and complex tasks, such as threat intelligence analysis, incident response planning, and security awareness training.

Improving Efficiency and Effectiveness: Automation reduces human error and improves the speed and efficiency of security operations. This enables security teams to respond to threats faster, prevent breaches more effectively, and improve overall security posture.

5. Network Security:

Network Traffic Analysis: AI algorithms can analyze network traffic data, identifying suspicious activity patterns that could indicate malicious activity. This includes detecting malware communication, identifying botnet activity, and identifying unauthorized access attempts. By analyzing

network traffic in real time, AI can help organizations to prevent attacks and mitigate the impact of incidents.
Adaptive Security Controls: AI can be used to create adaptive security controls that dynamically adjust based on changing network conditions and threat intelligence. This enables organizations to react quickly to evolving threats and adapt their security posture accordingly.

6. Data Security and Privacy:

Data Classification and Labeling: AI algorithms can analyze data content to classify it based on sensitivity and regulatory compliance requirements. This helps organizations to identify and protect sensitive data, reducing the risk of data breaches and non-compliance.
Privacy-Preserving Analytics: AI can be used to perform data analysis in a way that preserves privacy. Techniques like differential privacy and federated learning enable organizations to gain insights from data without compromising the privacy of individuals.

Challenges and Considerations:

While the benefits of AI in cybersecurity are numerous, it is important to acknowledge the challenges and considerations associated with its implementation:

Data Bias and Training Data Quality: AI algorithms are only as good as the data they are trained on. If the training data is biased or incomplete, it can lead to inaccurate results and false positives. It is crucial to ensure that the data used to train AI models is representative, diverse, and free from biases.
Adversarial Attacks: AI systems can be susceptible to adversarial attacks, where attackers manipulate or poison the training data to compromise the AI model's performance.

Organizations need to implement robust defenses to protect their AI systems from these attacks.

Transparency and Explainability: AI models can be complex and opaque, making it difficult to understand how they arrive at their decisions. This lack of transparency can be a concern, especially in critical security applications. Efforts are underway to develop more transparent and explainable AI models, but this is an ongoing challenge.

Ethical Implications: The use of AI in cybersecurity raises ethical questions about privacy, surveillance, and potential bias. Organizations need to consider these implications and ensure that AI is used responsibly and ethically.

The Future of AI in Cybersecurity:

The future of AI in cybersecurity holds immense promise. As AI technology continues to advance, we can expect to see even more sophisticated and effective AI-powered security solutions. Here are some key trends to watch:

Increased Adoption: The adoption of AI in cybersecurity is expected to grow rapidly in the coming years, as organizations realize the potential of these technologies to enhance security posture and reduce risk.

AI-Driven Threat Intelligence: AI will play an even more prominent role in threat intelligence, enabling organizations to identify and respond to emerging threats more effectively.

Automated Security Operations: AI will continue to automate security tasks, freeing up security professionals to focus on more strategic and complex activities.

AI-Enhanced Security Training: AI will be used to personalize security training and simulations, providing more effective and engaging learning experiences for security professionals.

Conclusion:

AI and automation are transforming the cybersecurity landscape, providing organizations with new tools and capabilities to combat evolving threats. However, it is crucial to embrace these technologies responsibly, addressing the challenges and ethical considerations associated with their use. By leveraging the power of AI and automation, organizations can build more resilient and proactive security defenses, ensuring a more secure digital future for all.

A Vision for a Secure Digital Future

The tapestry of our digital lives is woven with threads of convenience, connection, and innovation. Yet, this very fabric is susceptible to the insidious forces of cybercrime, threatening to unravel the very essence of our digital existence. As we venture deeper into a world increasingly reliant on technology, the need for robust cybersecurity becomes paramount.

The future of cybersecurity is not merely about building walls and moats around our digital domains; it's about fostering a culture of vigilance and resilience, where technology acts as a shield, not a barrier. It's about envisioning a future where every individual, every organization, and every nation is empowered to navigate the digital landscape with confidence, free from the shadows of cyber threats.

This vision, however, requires a paradigm shift in our approach to cybersecurity. We must move beyond the reactive, patchwork methods of the past and embrace a proactive, holistic strategy that anticipates threats, anticipates vulnerabilities, and adapts to the ever-changing landscape of cybercrime.

At the heart of this vision lies the integration of artificial intelligence (AI) and automation into our cybersecurity defenses. AI, with its ability to analyze vast amounts of data, identify patterns, and predict threats, can serve as an early warning system, detecting anomalies and potential attacks before they materialize. This predictive power allows for preemptive action, minimizing the impact of cyber incidents and mitigating potential damage.

Automation, too, plays a vital role in this future. By automating routine tasks, such as vulnerability scanning and incident response, security professionals can focus their expertise on strategic initiatives and complex challenges. This frees up valuable resources and allows for a more efficient allocation of manpower.

Imagine a future where AI-powered systems constantly monitor our networks, identifying and responding to threats in real time, even before human intervention is required. Imagine a future where security audits are conducted automatically, flagging potential vulnerabilities and recommending remediation strategies, ensuring that our systems are always kept up-to-date.

This vision also demands a collaborative effort across all sectors of society. Governments, businesses, and individuals must work together to establish robust cybersecurity frameworks, share best practices, and foster a culture of cybersecurity awareness. This collaborative spirit will ensure that everyone, from the individual user to the multinational corporation, is equipped to navigate the digital world with confidence and security.

The future of cybersecurity is not a distant dream; it's a reality we can shape. By embracing a proactive, technology-driven approach and fostering a collaborative spirit, we can build a digital future where security is not an afterthought but an integral part of our digital lives. A future where the shadows of cybercrime are replaced by the unwavering light of digital resilience.

This vision requires a fundamental shift in our mindset. We must move away from the perception of cybersecurity as a technical field solely for experts and recognize its profound impact on every aspect of our lives. The future of cybersecurity demands a collective effort, a shared responsibility to protect our digital world and safeguard the technologies that shape our future.

To realize this vision, we must invest in the next generation of cybersecurity professionals. By providing them with the knowledge, skills, and ethical framework necessary to navigate the ever-evolving landscape of cybercrime, we can ensure that our digital future is secure. We must nurture a culture of innovation, where creativity and ingenuity are harnessed to develop cutting-edge security solutions.

This is not merely a vision of the future, but a call to action. As we stand at the crossroads of technological advancement and potential cyber vulnerability, the path forward is clear: embrace a proactive, collaborative, and technologically driven approach to cybersecurity. Only then can we truly secure our digital future and unlock the boundless potential of the digital world.

The future of cybersecurity is not about fear, but about empowerment. It's about recognizing the power of technology to not only connect us but also protect us. It's about creating a digital ecosystem where innovation and security go hand-in-hand, where the boundless possibilities of the digital world are unlocked without the fear of cyber threats.

The future is within our grasp. It's time to embrace the vision of a secure digital future, a future where the shadows of cybercrime are banished by the unwavering light of digital resilience. It's time to build a future where every click, every connection, and every digital interaction is protected.

Acknowledgments

This book would not have been possible without the unwavering support and guidance of many remarkable individuals. First and foremost, I extend my deepest gratitude to Kevin Mitnick, my mentor, friend, and an inspiration to me throughout my journey. Your knowledge, wisdom, and unwavering belief in my abilities have shaped me into the cybersecurity professional I am today.

I am also eternally grateful to my family for their constant encouragement and love. My grandparents, Juana C. Lozano and Robert Lozano, have instilled in me the importance of perseverance and the pursuit of excellence. My siblings, Jennifer Martinez, my wife and kids Monica Gonzalez, Draven Trevino, Madison Trevino, Emma Trevino, Miranda Perez, Everlynn Trevino, have always been my steadfast supporters, offering a listening ear and a shoulder to lean on.

A special thanks to Ben Neece and Richard E. Zayas. Your insights, contributions, and unwavering belief in my vision have made this book a reality.

I would also like to acknowledge the contributions of Ben Neece and Victor Maldonado who have played a significant role in shaping my cybersecurity journey.

Finally, I express my gratitude to all the readers who embark on this journey with me. Your interest and support are what drive me to share my knowledge and experiences.

Appendix

The appendix provides a collection of resources and tools that complement the information discussed in the book.

Glossary of Cybersecurity Terms: A comprehensive list of common cybersecurity terms and their definitions.

Ethical Hacking Tools and Resources: A curated list of open-source and commercial tools used by ethical hackers for penetration testing and vulnerability assessment.

Security Best Practices and Standards: A collection of security guidelines, standards, and frameworks relevant to cybersecurity professionals.

Cybersecurity Blogs and Forums: A curated list of reputable blogs and forums dedicated to cybersecurity news, research, and discussions.

Online Security Training and Certification Programs: A list of accredited online training programs and certifications in cybersecurity.

Glossary

Backdoor: A hidden method for accessing a computer system or network without authorization.

Cybercrime: Criminal activity conducted through the use of computers and the internet.

Exploit: A piece of software designed to take advantage of a vulnerability in a system or application.

Firewall: A security system that monitors incoming and outgoing network traffic and blocks unauthorized access.

Hacker: An individual who uses their technical skills to gain unauthorized access to computer systems or networks.

Malicious Software (Malware): Software designed to harm or disrupt computer systems, including viruses, worms, and Trojans.

Network Security: Measures taken to protect computer networks from unauthorized access, use, disclosure, disruption, modification, or destruction.

Penetration Testing (Pen Testing): A simulated attack on a computer system or network to identify vulnerabilities and weaknesses.

Phishing: A type of social engineering attack that attempts to deceive users into revealing sensitive information.

Remote Code Execution (RCE): A vulnerability that allows an attacker to execute arbitrary code on a remote system.

Social Engineering: The art of manipulating people into performing actions that they would not normally do, often to gain access to sensitive information or systems.

Vulnerability: A weakness or flaw in a system or application that can be exploited by an attacker.

Zero-Day Exploit: An exploit that takes advantage of a vulnerability that has not been patched or addressed by the vendor.

References

Website: https://www.cosmoexploitgroupllc.com/
Email: info@cosmoexploitgroupllc.com

Cosmo Exploit Group - Reshaping the Cybersecurity
Business Environment

Author Biography

Michael Anthony Trevino Jr. is a renowned cybersecurity expert, ethical hacker, and former red teamer with extensive experience in the field. He is a passionate advocate for building strong cyber defenses and empowering individuals and organizations to navigate the ever-evolving digital landscape.

Michael's journey into cybersecurity began under the tutelage of legendary hacker Kevin Mitnick. He honed his skills in crafting custom zero-day exploits, including remote code execution vulnerabilities and zero-click exploits targeting mobile devices. His expertise has been instrumental in helping companies identify and mitigate vulnerabilities, building robust security postures.

Beyond his technical skills, Michael is deeply committed to ethical hacking practices, recognizing the importance of responsible and ethical conduct in the cybersecurity realm. He is a sought-after speaker at industry conferences and a frequent contributor to publications on cybersecurity.

Michael's book, "Shadows and Shields," reflects his personal experiences, insights, and dedication to protecting the digital world. He is driven by a desire to share his knowledge and inspire the next generation of cybersecurity professionals.